REIGNITING THE SPARK

Why Stable Relationships Lose Intimacy and How to Get It Back

DR. BRUCE CHALMER

TCK PUBLISHING.COM

ISBN: 978-1-63161-079-0

Sign up for Dr. Bruce Chalmer's newsletter at
www.askdrchalmer.brucechalmer.com

Published by TCK Publishing
www.TCKpublishing.com

Get discounts and special deals on our best selling books at
www.TCKpublishing.com/bookdeals

Check out additional discounts for bulk orders at
www.TCKpublishing.com/bulk-book-orders

CONTENTS

INTRODUCTION

RELATIONSHIPS IN SEVEN WORDS

Why Read This Book?

If you're in a committed relationship that you'd like to improve, then this book is for you.

Maybe you're considering couples therapy and wondering how it could help. Or, perhaps you've already done some couples therapy, but you wish it would help more. Maybe you don't know what to do, but you know that something in your relationship—your ability to communicate, your once passionate sex life, your sense of shared values and shared dreams—just isn't working anymore, and it hurts. Maybe your relationship is fine as it is, but you'd like to find new ways to deepen your intimate connection. This book is for you.

In these pages, you'll find a message of hope. This book won't solve your problems or enrich your relationship all on its own—that will require the efforts of both you and your partner. But it *will* strengthen your faith and help you understand the work that needs to be done.

The Seven Words

Years ago, when I was relatively new in private practice, a colleague in a consultation group asked me, "How do you do couples therapy, anyway?" I realized his question wasn't entirely serious, but I thought for a moment before answering, "I suppose when you boil it down, I'm basically telling people, 'Be kind and don't panic.'" Not long after, I realized I needed to expand the formula slightly, so I revised it to, "Be kind, don't panic, and have faith." Seven words (don't forget to count "and") that comprise three principles.

I've been working as a therapist for couples, individuals, and families for almost thirty years. Turns out relationships are more complicated than what seven words can capture—who knew? But the seven-word formula has continued to guide my work. And many of the couples I work with tell me that it has guided them, too.

I've been trained in quite a few techniques and schools of therapy over the years, including psychodynamic, narrative, cognitive behavioral, solution-focused, hypnotherapy, and others. I've learned a lot from those trainings and have applied those lessons to my work. Theoretical understandings are important guides, and techniques can be effective tools.

But somehow, the real people I see in my office often refuse to behave like the examples in my trainings. That's because life is more complex than what any school of thought or set of techniques can capture. And the longer I've practiced, the more I've realized that those seven words can be more beneficial to couples than any particular therapeutic technique.

Therefore, I've assiduously avoided creating yet another TLA (three-letter acronym) to brand my methodology. You don't need to sign up for my patented miracle cure or find a therapist trained in my institute.

Instead, this book uses the principles in the seven-word formula as a guide. We'll discuss what being a couple is all about, what may lead you to relationship problems, and how you can heal from those problems. Reading this book will help you understand your situation, guide you toward solutions, and offer you hope.

In Part I, we'll discuss kindness in the context of building relationships, along with the two golden gifts relationships need to survive and thrive. Part II is about anxiety and its causes, including trauma. In particular, we'll see how anxiety affects passion in a couple. Part III explores the roles of faith and forgiveness in healing from problems in your relationship, both individually and as a couple. Part IV then applies these ideas to a variety of topics that couples might struggle with, including marriage, sex, infidelity, and breakups.

At the end of each chapter is a section called Reflections, which features a set of questions for you to consider. The questions will help you consolidate your understanding of each chapter, apply the concepts to your own life, and prepare for the next steps. For each set of reflections, I recommend you find a quiet place to sit, take a few deep, relaxing breaths, and then consider each of the questions. You might want to write down your responses, stream-of-consciousness style.

About the Couples in This Book

The couples I refer to in this book are all composites based on people I've worked with. Their stories are realistic in the sense that I've worked with actual people in similar situations, but names and details have been changed thoroughly.

The names I chose for my example couples are common among the population I work with in Vermont, which is mostly white and Christian (at least in background, if not in practice). I have worked with a more diverse clientele than these names might suggest, including people of color, Jews, Muslims, many people who don't identify with any particular religion, and people whose first language isn't English. Of course, I don't think the ideas in this book are relevant only for white English-speaking Christians, but I do need to recognize that most of my experiences have been with a particular population. For similar reasons, I didn't include any gay or lesbian couples among my examples, even though I've worked with quite a few. The overwhelming majority of the couples I work with are heterosexual, and I don't want my examples to imply otherwise. I believe much of what I say in this book can be helpful to people in non-heterosexual relationships, but I'm suspicious of books that claim general applicability, especially when their authors are in no position to say so from their own experiences. I think it's a more respectful stance to recognize my limitations.

About Me

Besides my decades of experience as a psychologist working with couples in Vermont, there are a few facts about me that I think will give you, the reader, a better sense of what shapes my views.

First, I am Jewish. When I moved to Vermont as a young man forty-seven years ago, I became particularly active in the Jewish community, often in leadership roles. I mention that because my approach to couples therapy is influenced greatly by Jewish sources and experiences.

You might wonder why, then, the vast majority of people I work with are non-Jewish, but that's largely because I can't work professionally with people I'm close to in other parts of my life. As you'll see in my discussion of faith in Chapter 7, my approach does not assume any particular religious orientation. But many of my clients, both religious and secular, have expressed appreciation for my willingness to discuss their spiritual lives, and my own faith has been an integral part of that willingness.

Another factoid about me that I think is relevant: before becoming a psychologist, I was a statistician in medical research at the University of Vermont. In fact, I wrote a statistics textbook that you can still purchase, though you'll have some difficulty using the included 5¼" floppy disk (Chalmer, 1986). My background as a statistician informs my understanding of science's role in how we make sense of the world, and how we can apply scientific findings to the practice of therapy.

These two influences—faith and science—are central to how I work. To paraphrase Rabbi Jonathan Sacks (2011), science tells us what reality *is*, and faith tells us what reality *means*. To work with people in pain and help them heal requires both science and faith, and this book reflects both perspectives.

A Talmudic Tale

The Talmud (*Shabbat* 31a) tells a story of a scoffer who came to the sage Hillel and challenged him to teach the entire Torah while he was standing on one foot. Hillel agreed, and said to him, "What is hateful to you, don't do to another. That is the whole Torah—the rest is commentary. Now go and learn."

To paraphrase Hillel: "Be kind, don't panic, and have faith. That's what you need to know about relationships—the rest is commentary. Now go and learn."

Let's go and learn.

PART I

BE KIND

CHAPTER 1

I AM MY BELOVED'S, AND MY BELOVED IS MINE

Dierdre and Patrick

Dierdre and Patrick walk in and sit on my sofa, which I notice seems smaller than usual. When Patrick crosses his legs, Dierdre pushes his foot away from her half of the sofa.

They're in their early forties, married seventeen years, with three school-age kids. Financially more or less okay, stable jobs, no serious medical issues, no history of physical violence. The kids are doing generally well. Their family backgrounds are similar: both Dierdre and Patrick have Irish American parents who have stayed married; both grew up as practicing Catholics in the Boston area, but now rarely go to church; and both were the first in their families to attend college, which is where they met. A job change brought them to Vermont ten years ago.

In another culture, their marriage might have been arranged by their families. From the time they met, it was clear to them and even to their friends that they were right for each other. They spoke a common language, shared many of the same values and assumptions, and enjoyed a lot of the same activities. Plus, their sexual chemistry was intense. They moved in together a few years after college and were married not long afterward.

Why are they here now, as opposed to six months ago or six months from now? This question often elicits stories of discovered infidelity, substance abuse that resulted in a DUI, or a crisis involving one of the kids or an elderly parent. But Dierdre said: "I just can't keep doing this.

It's not one thing in particular—I know Patrick is basically a good man. But we're living like roommates, and everything he does irritates me. I've turned into someone I don't want to be." Patrick nodded, and added, "I don't know what I'm supposed to do. I'm trying to do it right, but I can't seem to please her. I don't want to fight. Splitting up would be awful. But I don't know what else to do—she's constantly angry, and it's getting so I don't want to come home at the end of the day."

Edgar and Sharon

Edgar and Sharon were referred to me by a social worker after Sharon swallowed a handful of antidepressant pills. Sharon is fifty-eight, Edgar sixty-three, and in their forty years of marriage, nothing like this had ever happened before. They run the dairy farm that has been in Edgar's family for three generations. Sharon also works part time in a medical office doing administrative work. Both of their kids left Vermont after high school, and neither wants to come back to the farm.

Yes, Sharon had reported some anxiety to her primary physician over the years, but she never mentioned anything about feeling suicidal. No, she doesn't want to kill herself now, and she's not sure she did when she took the pills—she just remembers feeling desperate. "I couldn't talk to Edgar about it. He'd just tell me to snap out of it, like he does when I get upset about the jokes he makes to our friends about the stupid things I do. Why can't I take a joke? Like he says, he pokes fun at everyone. And he's always been a good husband. He's right—I just need to grow a thicker skin."

"Doc, I never meant to hurt her when I would poke fun," Edgar said. "Hell, I didn't know I was hurting her. She's everything to me. Why couldn't she tell me?"

Wilma and George

Wilma and George's mutual antipathy is visible, audible, and virtually palpable—the air hangs with it alongside the humidity on the August day of our meeting.

Their visit to the agency where I was interning had been mandated by family court, since they couldn't agree on a schedule for their two kids as part of their separation. The judge said they needed to try couples therapy in hopes of improving their communication as soon-to-be-divorced parents. Either of them could have declined to participate, but at the cost of being deemed uncooperative—so each of their lawyers advised them to go ahead.

I had worked with families involved in custody disputes before, where each parent claimed that the other was unfit, dangerous, or just not as good for the kids. But this was different. Both George and Wilma actually wanted joint custody. Neither wanted their kids to lose their relationships with the other. Neither was alleging abuse. They just couldn't stand each other.

"He never misses a chance to put his little blonde whore in my face," Wilma said. "When he brings the kids back he makes sure she's with them in the car. I swear he goes out of his way to piss me off. He canceled a visit with them when he went off to his booty call—they asked me where he went. What am I supposed to tell them—that their father thinks it's more important to screw that conniving bitch than to spend time with them?"

"Well, now you see why our marriage didn't work. Can you imagine living with that every day? You see how she uses the kids against me?" George waved his hand in the general direction of Wilma, without looking at her. "She knows plenty about being a conniving bitch, I can tell you that. Did she tell you she was having phone sex with her high school boyfriend at the same time she was getting all high and mighty about me?"

Kindness and Kinship

Why do we pair up in couples, anyway? Here's a reason—I think it's *the* reason: we couple for kindness. Or, if kindness isn't the reason we pair up in the first place, it's the reason we *stay* together if we have the choice. (There's research to back up that idea.[1]) Maybe we initially pair up for sex, procreation, social status, help with the demands of life, diversion from boredom or loneliness, or just because we're human

---

[1]See, for example, Smith (2014) for a summary of some of the relevant research.

and coupling is what our species does. But we stay coupled because of kindness—and uncouple (when we can) for a lack of kindness.

Kindness isn't merely being pleasant to others, or serving their needs, or even putting their needs before your own. You can do all those things in a subservient relationship, out of a sense of civic-mindedness, or as an expression of a religious calling. You can and should do good deeds for employers and employees, neighbors, or even strangers, but that sort of kindness is not what keeps people together as a couple.

Rather, the kindness that keeps people in a relationship comes when each partner treats the other as one of their kin, which is to say, one of their kind (the words are from the same root).[2] To be kind is to recognize not only a common humanity, but a familial bond. What will keep you together in a couple is the sense of being a unit, rather than two individuals. While falling in love is initially about attraction and passionate desire, the love that keeps you coupled over the long term is about shared kinship. As Song of Songs expresses it: "I am my beloved's and my beloved is mine."[3] As romantic as that sounds, that sort of kindness also extends to when my beloved is annoying the crap out of me.[4] You may be a pest, but you're *my* pest, and I'm yours. That's the sense of kinship that keeps people coupled. (That's also why marriage is such a significant step, as we'll discuss in Chapter 10.)

Of course, people can and sometimes do treat their kin horribly, and we don't describe that as kindness. And many people are effectively trapped in those relationships, since trying to get out could get them killed, maimed, or left destitute. If that's you, you don't need kindness, but escape. You don't need couples therapy either. You need a safety plan—seek help immediately.

But I've met many others who knew that they *could* get out of an abusive relationship without risking life, limb, or livelihood, yet nevertheless stayed. It's the fear of losing kinship—as well as the hope that kindness brings, even if it's been accompanied by abuse or betrayal—that keeps those people in otherwise bad relationships. The "hearts and flowers" behavior that abusers often exhibit after an

---

[2] Cf. Hamlet's first line in the play (Act 1, scene 2), referring to his uncle/stepfather as "A little more than kin, and less than kind."

[3] Song of Songs 6:3

[4] Note to *my* beloved: Never you!

explosion reinforces this phenomenon, as it serves to remind the victim that the abuser is capable of showing kindness.

Just as kindness keeps people in good relationships and fear of its loss keeps them in bad ones, fear of losing kindness also stops many people from coupling up in the first place. To fear commitment is to fear establishing a kinship bond. The stereotypical commitment-phobe may seem like he wants to remain in eternal adolescence. Yet many of the commitment-fearing men (and occasional women) whom I've met fear commitment not because they're having too much fun being single, but because they've witnessed their parents' repeated couplings and uncouplings, or because they've been abused as young children, or because they've been hurt before in previous relationships. They can't trust that the love based on kinship can be anything but painful and ultimately futile. They're in my office, alone or with frustrated partners, because they *do* want kinship, and they want to believe it's possible— but taking that risk terrifies them.

The three couples I introduced at the beginning of this chapter were dealing with failures of kindness. Sometimes it's not subtle, as with Wilma and George, the couple who wanted joint custody of their kids. They were nursing a deep sense of betrayal toward each other, and they had each done the other wrong by acts of disloyalty. This sense of betrayed kinship triggers a powerful mechanism of disgust, the sort of contempt we reserve for traitors as opposed to mere enemies. Wilma and George were finished as kin with each other; my work with them would be to foster enough sense of shared humanity that they could each tolerate their children's kinship with the other parent.

But the failure of kindness isn't always so blatant. Sharon, whose husband would constantly poke fun at her, largely blamed herself for not having a thicker skin. She thought of Edgar as a good husband, and his dismissal of her pain left her feeling crazy: *He's a good husband, so if I'm hurting like this it's not that he's being mean; it must be because I'm too sensitive.* Both Sharon and Edgar shared that understanding, and Edgar reinforced it every time he minimized Sharon's objections. For Sharon to insist that Edgar change his behavior would have required a willingness to risk the marriage. That thought was no more available to her—or to him for that matter—than the thought of disowning their children. She risked death, by attempting suicide, rather than risk the marriage by confronting Edgar.

The lack of kindness in Sharon and Edgar's marriage wasn't as obvious as George and Wilma's infidelity, but it was destructive nonetheless.

Dierdre and Patrick's story is less dramatic, but very common in my practice. There was no one act of betrayal or desperation. Yet a marriage that had been founded on strong mutual attraction and shared values had somehow devolved into a prison. Differences between them that once seemed charming, or at least manageable, now grated on Dierdre. And Patrick's efforts to change for her never seemed to help. Coming into each other's presence felt more and more like a high-stakes trial, rather than a relaxing homecoming. Like Sharon and Edgar, Dierdre and Patrick still felt a bond of kinship, but their increasing misery threatened that bond. And unlike Sharon and Edgar, Dierdre and Patrick were willing to consider splitting up, rather than continue living together in misery—which meant that neither spouse was suicidal, but the marriage might well have been. The remaining hope of finding their kindness again was what brought them to my office.

The Assumption of Good Will

If we stay in relationships for kindness—that particular form of kindness expressed as "I am my beloved's and my beloved is mine"— then the tipping point for a couple comes when they no longer experience their partner as their own. If you're mine, and I'm yours, we're part of each other. As I mentioned before, this isn't just about the romantic attraction that (often) dominates the early stages of a relationship, when everything your beloved does is awe-inspiring. The feeling of mutual belonging that keeps people together over the long haul is one that stands up to irritation, anxiety, and conflict.

That sense of belonging—of familial and tribal loyalty—is a basic component of our psychological makeup.[5] In particular, when I experience your actions toward me, how I interpret those actions will depend greatly on whether I consider you "mine" or not. If you're mine, I'm much more willing to assume that your actions are based on something positive—or at least not intentionally hostile—than if you're

---

[5] See Jonathan Haidt's book *The Righteous Mind* (2012). Haidt describes how a set of innate "modules" that evolved as adaptations to problems of survival have combined in different cultures to shape our moral judgments and ethical behaviors.

not mine. In other words, if you're mine, I'll assume good will. If you're smiling and friendly, that's easy, but I'll also tend to assume good will even if you're upset, in that I'll ascribe your being upset to pain rather than hostility.[6] My inclination will be to help you feel better, rather than to defend myself from your aggression. You're mine, and I'm yours.

One of the hallmarks of a couple who is glad to be in their relationship is that they both assume good will a lot.[7] And it's not merely that they assume good will when they see their partner looking happy—they tend to assume good will even when their partner is in distress. They'll show a strong bias toward assuming something positive when it comes to their partner's behavior; the magic of this, of course, is that the more I interpret my partner's intentions as positive, the more my behavior will push her to see *my* intentions as positive, and the virtuous cycle reinforces both of our perceptions that we belong to each other, resulting in an even stronger assumption of good will, and on and on.

The acid test of assuming good will in a relationship comes when one partner (say, a wife) is in distress not because of some external event, but because of something the other partner (say, a husband) did. And that's when the true power of the assumption of good will comes through. If the wife assumes good will from her husband, she'll tend to express her distress in terms of what hurts and what she'd like her husband to do differently, rather than attacking his character or motives. If the husband assumes good will from his wife, he'll tend to listen carefully to what she says with concern and respect, rather than dismissiveness, and he will respond helpfully instead of defensively.[8]

---

[6] As I write this, two attacks in the United States have occurred within days. The first involved a Muslim immigrant using a truck to kill people on a bicycle path in New York City, and the second a locally-born white man who had been discharged from the Air Force, shooting people in a church in Texas. The public reactions to these events from the president were, respectively, to call for increased restrictions on immigration to prevent radicals from entering the country, and to attribute the shooting to mental health issues. Within the tribe, we see pain to be treated, rather than evil to be excluded.

[7] John Gottman (2015), referring to the work of Robert Weiss, calls this "positive sentiment override." Gottman's research on couples shows that members of happy couples tend to perceive each other's behaviors as more positive—and hold on to that perception longer—than do members of couples headed for divorce.

[8] This corresponds directly to Gottman's (2015) findings in his research on newlyweds. In heterosexual couples, if a complaint is to be raised, it's usually the woman who raises it. Two features (among others) distinguish the happy couples in Gottman's research from the couples destined for divorce: (1) when the woman raises the complaint, she does so gently rather than harshly, and (2) the man frequently accepts influence from the woman. These features are mutually reinforcing.

What You Assume Changes What Happens

The assumption of good will is essentially a perceptual bias. It doesn't make you a more *accurate* interpreter of someone's motives; it just makes you a more *generous* interpreter of someone's motives.[9] In fact, that positive bias probably makes you *less* accurate in some circumstances.[10]

But how you interpret your partner's behavior has a profound effect on your relationship. If you tend to assume that your partner means ill for you, your reactions will make this more likely to be true, even if it wasn't true at first. And if you tend to assume good will from your partner—even if you're wrong about it sometimes—your reactions will push your communication in a more positive direction.[11]

By the time I met Wilma and George, they had long since lost any assumption of good will. Wilma was certain that George was intentionally trying to piss her off by bringing his girlfriend in the car, and George was certain that Wilma's objections about canceled visits were her way of using the kids against him.

But what if Wilma imagined that George had a more innocent motive for having his girlfriend in the car? What if she considered the possibility, for example, that the girlfriend was looking for an opening to meet Wilma in hopes of developing a workable relationship? Wilma might then be able to manage a polite greeting, and they might then go on to establish some rapport. This could happen even if the girlfriend had no such intention to start with.

And what if George could have listened seriously to Wilma's concerns about the kids' disappointment when he canceled visits? What if he could notice that, angry as she was, Wilma didn't want to badmouth him to the kids, she just wanted them to have a good relationship with him? He might have been able to consider her

---

[9]In working with couples, I often question the very idea of accuracy with respect to motives, since so much of what determines behavior is unconscious, and mixed feelings are the rule rather than the exception.

[10]Indeed, our perception of someone as in- or out-group affects our judgments of facts. See, e.g., Washburn & Skitka (2017).

[11]This can be problematic if your partner is a sociopath and really does mean you harm, in that your positive bias could make it harder for you to perceive your partner's evil intention. That same positive bias can also lead you to tolerate repeated abuse. The assumption of good will doesn't mean that you should stay in the relationship.

concerns respectfully, and Wilma might have responded in a way that reduced their mutual animosity.

For Wilma and George to imagine benign intentions behind the other's behavior was especially difficult, because they weren't merely disappointing or hurting each other—theirs was the pain of betrayal. Most of us can forgive moments of selfish unkindness from our kin (as well as from outsiders). But to forgive betrayal—behavior that calls into question someone's loyalty, often involving duplicity and deception— is a lot harder. It's not impossible to forgive betrayal, but it's difficult. And even when the betrayed partner can forgive, the relationship will usually end anyway, because it's a lot harder to view someone as kin once they've betrayed you. The couples that survive betrayal are the ones that can find a shared understanding, and even an appreciation, of the growth that they experience after the crisis. Wilma and George were nowhere near a shared understanding of their mutual betrayals.

Edgar and Sharon's problem wasn't that they lacked the assumption of good will; rather, their problem was that they assumed good will too readily. They knew, without a doubt, that they were kin to each other, and neither could interpret the other's behavior as threatening to that bond. Had Sharon been able to see Edgar's dismissiveness as cruel (even if unconsciously so), she might have directed her anger at him instead of herself. Instead of being suicidal, she might have put the marriage on the line by insisting that Edgar change his behavior.

But just as Sharon couldn't see Edgar's behavior as cruel, neither could Edgar. All he could see was that she was too sensitive—which he regularly reminded her—and ultimately that her act of despair must be evidence of mental illness. In that interpretation, he was supported not only by Sharon herself, but by the mental health system that got involved when Sharon took the pills (and, more generally, by cultural assumptions that women who object to men's behavior are bitchy, mean, or crazy).

After a session and a half of deconstructing all of this, Sharon was still sad, and Edgar said to me in frustration, "Doc, just tell me what to do!" I was taken aback by the request, not only because I was new to private practice and was taken aback quite frequently, but also because I felt (and still feel) utterly unqualified to tell someone what to do. But there it was—he'd had enough theorizing. So I said, "Just be nice to her."

"Be nice to her? You mean not poking fun at her?"

"Right. Don't poke fun at her. Listen to what she says."

When they came back two weeks later, Sharon was beaming. "He's being nice to me. He asks how I feel about things. I love it." Edgar seemed relieved. The irony of all this was not lost on me: Edgar had ignored and trivialized Sharon's objections for years, but readily listened to a male "Doc." And Sharon, instead of being supremely angered by this turn of events (as often happens), was simply relaxed and happy. She didn't want to deconstruct sexism any more than Edgar did; she just wanted him to be kind.

For Dierdre and Patrick, the work wasn't so simple. Dierdre knew she was being unkind to Patrick, but her efforts to be nicer felt phony. The more he tried to please her, the more she felt pressured, and the more he was frustrated, the more his efforts seemed manipulative rather than sincere. By the time they came to therapy, they were locked in a cycle of mutually reinforcing misery.

As Dierdre put it, "I wish I wanted to be with Patrick, but I don't know how to do that anymore." She felt guilty about the sort of person she had become in her constant irritation at her husband, but she was also determined to not suppress her feelings just to stay with him. She'd seen too many women do that, including her own mother. Patrick was both hurt and mystified. He'd thought he'd been doing what a husband should do, but somehow it wasn't right.

Each of them wanted to trust the other's good will, but they had been inadvertently training each other to expect hurt in their interactions. Their challenge would be to tolerate the pain and anxiety long enough to discover the power they each had to change the pattern.

Almost all the couples I see for therapy started out assuming good will from each other.[12] What usually brings them to my office is that they lost that assumption and are questioning whether they can still trust each other as kin. They're wondering how they lost it—and even more, they're wondering how or if they can get it back. And by the time they come to therapy, they've usually been trying for years.[13]

---

[12]I say "almost" because I've met couples whose marriages were arranged for them, were the result of an unplanned pregnancy, or were means of escape from danger and they didn't know each other enough to form an assumption of good will at first.

[13]According to a 1992 study by Jane Buongiorno and Clifford Notarius (1992) frequently cited by John Gottman, the average wait time before couples in their study came to therapy was about six years. I've been unable to find a more recent study. In my own clinical experience there's a lot of variability, but when I ask couples why they're here now as opposed to six months ago or six months from now, they often say things like, "In hindsight, we should have come in years ago."

Reflections: I Am My Beloved's, and My Beloved Is Mine

1. We talked in this chapter about kindness being more than just treating others well. It means treating others as kin—as members of your tribe. Think of the people in your life whom you consider your kin in some way. This can include family, but also wider circles such as fellow members of a religion, ethnicity, or political affiliation. Focus on two or three people of varying degrees of closeness to you, including your spouse or partner if you have one. How did each one get to be your kin? Was it through birth, choice, or some other way? If you chose the person, when did you first sense that they had become your kin? What reassures you that they are still kin to you? What do you do to reassure them? How do you know they're kin even when you're in some kind of conflict with them?

2. Recall a time when one of those people seemed to be angry. If you can, remember your first emotional reactions—did you feel compassionate, afraid, angry, or some other emotions? How did you respond? Now imagine or recall a similar expression of anger from someone outside your kinship circle—perhaps something you saw in the news. How does kinship (or its lack) affect your response?

3. Can you think of a time when your response to someone's anger helped calm them? What did you do that helped? How were you able to be helpful rather than hostile? How about a time when someone else's response to your anger helped calm you down? What did they do that helped?

4. Now focus on your relationship with a partner (present, past, or imagined). Think of a time when the relationship was going well, and recall (or imagine) a moment when the two of you were together. What was happening that you felt good about, that made you glad to be in the relationship? More generally, what's important to you in a relationship?

CHAPTER 2

THE TWO GOLDEN GIFTS

Stability and Intimacy

Tara and Trey come to me because they want to stay together, but they keep repeating a cycle of splitting up and getting back together. It's gone on like that for three years. They clearly love each other, and they tell me they have an active sex life, but they can't manage to stay together for more than a year or so before one of them calls it quits, often during a screaming argument fueled by drinking. Then within a few weeks, or at most a few months, they get back together, and the cycle repeats. This has happened four times now.

Doris and Ken come to me because they also want to stay together, but their story is very different. They've been married for thirty-five years and have four adult kids and seven grandchildren. What brought them to therapy was Ken's discovery of Doris's text messages with an old high school boyfriend. The texts had gone from friendly to emotional to sexual over the course of a few weeks. Doris insists there's been no physical contact with the old boyfriend—he lives far away—and Ken is pretty sure he believes her, although there was at least one opportunity he knows of when they could have been together. But this event has shaken them both—Ken, because he had never doubted Doris's faithfulness, and Doris, because she never thought herself capable of straying even as much as she did. They also clearly love each other, and a year ago both would have said they had a solid marriage.

Though there are endless variations, Tara and Trey and Doris and Ken illustrate the two golden gifts you need to assume good will in a relationship. I mean the kind of gifts we refer to when we talk about someone who's become highly skilled at something: you need some basic talent, but then you need to develop your talent into skill and mastery.

So what are the two golden gifts? Let's call them stability and intimacy. You need to get good at both if you want your relationship to work. And the funny thing about the two gifts is that sometimes they work together, but sometimes they conflict: your work to develop one makes it harder to hang on to the other, which is why long-term relationships can be so challenging to maintain.

Stability Skills Are About Lowering Anxiety

Stability is the gift that Tara and Trey were struggling with. Stability skills are all about building a sense of confidence in each other and in the relationship. You come to know what helps your partner feel good, and you learn how to comfort them when they're upset or sad. You show up when you're needed. You do your part to keep the bills paid, the house in decent order, and the kids picked up and dropped off. You're generally reliable, which means generally sober—substance abuse can wreak havoc on reliability.

Of course, a fundamental stability skill is fostering a trust that neither you nor your partner will be violent or use threats to intimidate each other. Sexual fidelity is another basic stability skill: you don't cheat, and you behave in ways that reassure your partner that you *won't* cheat. More generally, the gift of stability is the sense that you can count on each other. You develop the basic assumption of good will that we talked about in Chapter 1.

Tara and Trey's cycle started because they lacked that basic assumption of good will. They had each grown up in households with unstable relationships, in which arguments were frequent, volatile, and rarely ended in reconciliation. They were powerfully attracted to each other, but whenever a difference arose, it would escalate into a chain of accusations and counter-accusations, reinforcing their views that the other didn't care about them and that they just weren't on the same team.

Though it never got to the point of physical violence, their arguments would often lead one or the other to declare that the relationship was over. The more frequent these arguments became, the less they trusted each other's good will.

This would lead them to split up, and often one or both would quickly enter another relationship, since they were seeking a distraction from the pain and anxiety of breaking up. The new relationships wouldn't last—not surprisingly, because Trey and Tara still contacted each other—and they'd find themselves together again. And the cycle would repeat, not only because the same triggers were always present, but also because they could no longer trust each other's fidelity.

Essentially, stability skills are all about lowering anxiety—both your own and your partner's. Neither Tara nor Trey had grown up seeing adults do that very often, and they never learned how to calm themselves or each other when they needed to. Alcohol, their go-to method for calming themselves, just upped the ante by leaving them both less capable of hearing each other and more prone to uninhibited reactions—hence the nasty fights.

Notice that stability for Tara and Trey wouldn't necessarily keep them together; rather, it would help them to finally escape their cycle. Stability would mean that their relationship would stop driving them nuts, whether they ended up together or not.

It's Not About Communication Skills

Like most couples who come to see me, Tara and Trey said that were looking for a better way of communicating. After all, they kept breaking up in the midst of arguments, which seemed to solve nothing and left them both frustrated and hurt. Could they find tools for improving their communication skills, so they could solve their problems instead of turning them into arguments? Wouldn't that give them a better chance at a stable relationship?

A Google search for "tools to improve communication skills" turned up over fifty million results, so there's no lack of available resources. But, also like most couples who come to me, Tara and Trey's problem wasn't a lack of communication skills. Their problem was *what* they thought and felt, not *how* they communicated it.[14] What they thought and felt was essentially "I don't trust you," and they communicated that very clearly. Communication techniques such as "I" statements, active listening, restatements, and the like wouldn't have made it any clearer.

The problem with techniques is that when you're freaking out, the portion of your brain that can remember and implement the technique isn't available. And when you're calm, the technique isn't necessary (and feels awkward to boot). As I noted above, the issue you're having with your partner usually isn't that you're failing to communicate clearly; it's that you're communicating something painful, scary, or offensive.

Couples often seek a set of rules for handling arguments that seem to be heading out of control. Again, there are countless versions of such rules available online, and the same problem applies: when your anxiety level passes a critical point, you can't remember the rules because your midbrain (the part that mostly controls your behavior in fight-or-flight situations) doesn't know them, and the part of your brain that does know them is offline.

The rules for fair fighting are often great descriptions of how a well-functioning couple communicates in times of disagreement: no blaming, no yelling, no insulting language, no responding without first checking that they've understood their partner, and so on. Learning how well-functioning couples communicate can be a useful exercise, since it can help you to see both your helpful and unhelpful actions. (John Gottman's research is particularly relevant to this point.) But when couples try to apply the rules as a way of governing their fights, they sometimes just end up arguing about the rules and who's violating them more egregiously.

So what *does* support stability? What can a couple such as Tara and Trey do to escape the cycle of anxiety-fight-breakup-makeup?

---

[14]I've occasionally worked with people who actually did have difficulty communicating, usually because they were neuroatypical in some way. Sometimes this relates to meta-communication: for example, knowing that if your partner asks you a question, you need to say something to acknowledge your partner even if you don't know what to respond. In those situations, learning communications skills can help reduce misunderstandings.

The Key to Stability is Character

Stability is all about keeping your anxiety under control. As such, the key to stability isn't what your partner does or what the two of you do as a couple. The key to stability is getting control of yourself—that is, assuming responsibility for your own behavior, even when you're angry, frustrated, scared, or lonely—and even when your partner isn't cooperating.

That means that the key to stability is acting based on what's right, not how you feel. It's what every culture strives to teach its children: that the norms of good behavior need to take precedence over what you're feeling in the moment. Cultures differ considerably in their definitions of those norms, but the social approval and censure that uphold the norms are why cultures continue to exist. The very idea of a stable relationship is defined by those rules.

We describe people who consistently act admirably—i.e., according to the norms of good behavior—as being of good character.

The idea that you need to do what's right rather than act on your feelings doesn't sound like something a psychotherapist says. The culture of therapy for the past few decades has been centered on self-actualization: becoming and expressing your "authentic" self. This implies that staying true to your authentic self is a good thing, while failure to do so causes psychopathology and suffering.

This is particularly true of individual therapy, much of which is based on the idea that we need to get in touch with our true feelings. To enable this journey of discovery, psychotherapy provides a sacred space of confidentiality and a cocoon of unconditional positive regard from the therapist. In this way, clients can explore and reveal their darkest secrets without fear of judgment.[15]

But what if our authentic self is as prone to bad behavior as it is to good? As David Brooks discusses in his book *The Road to Character* (2015), the idea of trusting one's innermost self, rather than seeing it as a set of forces to be carefully regulated, is a recent development in human history. Earlier generations viewed character as the ability to rein in our innate capacity for evil and channel it toward good.

---

[15]Of course, there is a greatly reduced expectation of confidentiality for children, or more generally, anyone for whom therapy is mandated by others. For them, therapy is designed precisely to enforce behavioral norms, and is therefore all about stability.

Good character doesn't mean that someone blindly complies with cultural norms. In fact, we often come to admire people who seek changes to cultural norms in the name of a higher good.[16] But someone of good character is someone you are more likely to trust—even if you may disagree with them—because it's clear that their willingness to take an unpopular stand is principled, rather than driven by their own base urges. In other words, the essence of good character is selflessness, not self-actualization.

That's why character is the key to stability in relationships. Even if you disagree with your partner, good character allows for trust. And, conversely, that's why an exclusive focus on self-authenticity—as often happens in individual therapy—can be profoundly destabilizing to a relationship. Feelings change moment to moment, but character stands the test of time, which is why stability requires character.

Character is what Trey and Tara needed to develop in order to get them out of their cycle. When you can control your own reactions and trust that your partner can control theirs, stability becomes possible.

But . . .

Stability Alone Isn't Sufficient

Ken and Doris had stability skills pretty much down pat. Over the decades, they had learned to steer clear of each other's hot spots. They worked out their differences about money, kids, and household tasks, which wasn't that difficult, because they had their mutual expectations lined up pretty well. And they had had a comfortable sex life in earlier years, though more recently it had virtually disappeared.

So what made Doris threaten that stable, comfortable relationship with her texting? In some ways, she was as shocked as Ken that she had let it happen. But as we talked about it in therapy, she began to understand what made the lure of her old boyfriend's interest so compelling. When she reconnected with her old boyfriend, she felt herself come alive in ways she hadn't felt in years—ways she had thought were long gone. She realized how risky her continued texting was to her marriage, but she kept doing it anyway. And it wasn't until

---

[16]Such admiration usually comes later on, when the norms have shifted. Prophets aren't popular in their own day.

Ken found out about it—which, in hindsight, happened because she was all but screaming to be caught—that she realized her fascination wasn't about the old boyfriend, or even about deficiencies in Ken. She realized that she had been shutting down parts of herself for decades for the sake of stability in her marriage.

What Doris hungered for was intimacy: the experience of being emotionally present and honest with someone else doing the same. And, as she came to realize, she hadn't had much of that in her marriage for a very long time.

Doris and Ken had learned to avoid anything that might threaten their stability. Sometimes, this meant giving up what they wanted for the sake of peace, which is fine, unless what they're giving up is actually important. Without realizing it, Doris had been suppressing some important aspects of what she wanted because she sensed that they made Ken uneasy. And whatever Ken might have noticed about the slow decay of their relationship, he had filtered out of consciousness because it was too scary.

Lack of Intimacy Itself Becomes Destabilizing

Deprive an organism of its needs, and it will become sick.[17] Instability is relational sickness—too much of it and the relationship dies. You might think that by avoiding the anxiety of intimacy you will preserve stability, but your efforts will ultimately fail, because a lack of intimacy itself becomes destabilizing.

Why does this happen? Why did Doris continue to text her old boyfriend, knowing full well how risky it was to her marriage? Why do people who love their spouses and their marriages have affairs, or hide expenditures from their partner, or otherwise act in ways that undermine trust? You could say these are failures of character, in that they reflect people doing what they want to do instead of doing what's right, but that misses the point. Of course, deceiving your spouse is a failure of character, and it is profoundly destabilizing to a relationship.

---

[17] I realize this assertion is tautological: needs are, by definition, that which prevent an organism from becoming sick.

But why would someone like Doris, whose character had been consistently solid for decades, do what she did?

If stability provides the roots for a relationship, intimacy provides the energy for growth. Doris and Ken had developed a solid root structure for their marriage. They trusted themselves and each other, largely because neither one of them risked unpredictability. But the structure they had created and enforced on themselves became stultifying: they couldn't let themselves explore their own thoughts or desires for fear that they might upset their partner. This was reflected in the decline of their sex life.

Plant a healthy seed in a sufficiently hospitable environment, and it will sprout and push through anything to get what it needs, or it will die trying. Any organism is alive to the extent that it's trying to interact with its environment; otherwise it's dying or dead.

Intimacy is how people interact with the world to get what they need. Physically, we're wired to seek food, water, and shelter, and if we fail to act on those needs, we die. Emotionally, we're social creatures: we seek connection (sexual or otherwise), status, and social approval. If we're deprived of those things, we feel anxious and depressed. Spiritually, we're meaning-making creatures: we want our lives to feel meaningful in the context of greater realities, and we become anxious if they don't.[18]

To be intimate with the world is to act consistently on those physical, emotional, and spiritual needs. More specifically, to be intimate is to be open to what the world wants from you, and to act on what you want from the world. Intimacy is what gives you the feeling of being alive, because intimacy *is* being alive.[19] If you're denied that intimacy, you get sick. And when a relationship interferes with your ability to express intimacy, you'll act like a seed planted under a sidewalk: you'll press through, even if it means cracking the sidewalk to do it.

Just as each of us is an organism made up of internal systems that operate semi-independently from each other, a relationship

---

[18] The needs for social connection and spiritual meaning can also be explained in evolutionary terms at the level of groups (Haidt, 2012). Note, incidentally, that this understanding of needs is different from Maslow's needs-hierarchy construct in that it's not inherently hierarchical. People often sacrifice physical needs—even life itself—for meaning.

[19] As Sean D. Kelly (2017) noted, referring to the 17th century philosopher Blaise Pascal: "The goal of life, for Pascal, is not happiness, peace, or fulfillment, but *aliveness.*"

between two people can be viewed as a living organism separate from the individuals it comprises. And just as we each need stability and intimacy as individuals, so too do relationships. A relationship that is too sensitive to the partners' changing emotions will lurch from crisis to crisis, lacking the stability to survive. But a stable relationship that doesn't allow for growth and change—one that stifles intimacy—will also face an eventual crisis: it will either learn to adapt, or die.

Doris persisted in her texting because she felt alive—she felt intimately connected with herself and the world in a way she hadn't realized she was missing. But because she genuinely loved Ken, she didn't want to hurt him or destabilize their marriage by bringing it up. Years of avoiding anxiety-prone topics had trained both Doris and Ken to avoid talking about dissatisfaction, and even to avoid recognizing it. But like the seed pushing through concrete, Doris's need for intimacy led her to force the issue. Whether her getting caught was somehow intentional or not, the crisis pushed their marriage to either allow for intimacy or die.

Intimacy Skills Are About Tolerating Anxiety

As I noted earlier, stability skills are all about lowering anxiety: you behave in ways that reassure yourself and your partner, and you avoid doing things that might increase anxiety. Doris and Ken had learned early on—sometimes painfully—what their limits were, and their solid marriage was a testimony to their respect of those limits.

But intimacy requires a very different set of skills. Intimacy skills aren't about lowering anxiety; rather, intimacy requires that you tolerate, and sometimes even raise, anxiety. To risk genuine emotional honesty, and to be open to someone else's honesty, is often scary. And the more important that someone else is to you, the scarier intimacy can be. Ironically, it's often easier to be intimate with someone who's not particularly important to you than it is with your partner, the person with whom you're trying to build a stable life. That's why the pull of an affair can be so powerful: it gives free rein to your desire for intimacy, since you're not trying to build a life with an affair partner.

The paradox that many long-term couples encounter is that the more important their relationship becomes to them, the scarier intimacy can be. To express a hitherto hidden desire, raise a complaint about your partner's behavior, or even let yourself show unbridled joy and enthusiasm is to risk your partner's rejection, anger, or disconnection.

The key to developing intimacy in an important relationship—that is, a relationship for which you want long-term stability—is learning to tolerate the anxiety that comes with emotional honesty. This means not only a willingness to say what you need to say, but also a willingness to hear with an open heart what you might not want to hear.

Kindness Needs Both Stability and Intimacy

Kindness is what keeps couples together, but the two golden gifts of stability and intimacy are what make it *possible* to stay together. To retain that feeling of kinship, you need both the comfort of stability and the aliveness of intimacy.

For evidence of this, just consider what happens when you lack either one.

The roller-coaster instability of Tara and Trey's relationship was reflected in their frequent breakups, but also in their inability to trust each other's good will when they would reunite. Any moment of insecurity for one of them was apt to trigger anxiety in the other, even while each (consciously or not) was holding the other responsible for relieving their anxiety. Each was effectively saying, "If only you would be clear, unambiguous, and consistent in your loving behavior toward me, I wouldn't have to doubt you so much. But you keep doubting me!"

So, in addition to the differences that arose simply from being two different people, they were continually beset by doubts about each other's loyalty, which made them more suspicious of each other's motives. Their initial predilection to assume good will was eroded. Instead of seeing each other's moments of irritability as pain, thereby eliciting sympathy and comfort, they saw those moments as evidence of bad intent and disloyalty, thereby eliciting suspicion and hostility. They came to my office realizing that this pattern was unsustainable, but they were unclear on how to escape it.

For Doris and Ken, the problem was intimacy. They had been so successful in avoiding issues that might threaten their stability that they had effectively closed off emotional honesty between them. Instead of lurching from crisis to crisis, they had gradually shut down the parts of themselves that made them feel alive.

They maintained their assumption of each other's good will through a long marriage, but when Doris's texting came to light, everything was called into question. The lack of intimacy in their relationship had disrupted their sense of kinship. They came to my office wondering if their marriage could recover.

For both couples—indeed, for most of the couples I see—the problem is that the lack of stability, lack of intimacy, or both diminishes their kindness toward themselves and each other. If they could calm themselves enough to foster stability, or tolerate the anxiety enough to risk intimacy, they might be able to return to the sense of kinship that brought them together. But the anxiety often overwhelms them.

In other words, the problem is panic.

Reflections: The Two Golden Gifts

1. Let's revisit a question from Chapter 1. Focus on your relationship with a partner (present, past, or imagined). Think of a time when the relationship was going well, and recall (or imagine) a moment when the two of you were together. What was happening that you felt good about, that made you glad to be in the relationship?

2. Remembering that same moment, what was happening that reassured you that the relationship was stable? What was happening that gave you an experience of intimacy?

3. Now recall or imagine a time when the relationship was not going well. What was causing you distress? How did the problems you were having affect the stability of the relationship? How did the problems affect intimacy in the relationship?

4. Have you ever had times when you've wanted to discuss something with your partner, but haven't because you were worried about how your partner would react?

PART II

DON'T PANIC

CHAPTER 3

PANIC AND ITS EFFECTS (GOOD AND BAD)

Why Do We Panic?

Evolution selects for survival. Those ancient people who didn't panic[20] sufficiently when they encountered a saber-toothed tiger for the second time, having survived a close call, didn't live to become our ancestors. In fact, those who survived best tended to panic at just the hint of a saber-toothed tiger in the vicinity.

Of course, simply freaking out emotionally doesn't confer much in the way of survival advantage. It's what we do when we panic, not how we feel, that makes the difference. The physiology of panic is all about escaping a dangerous predator. If the situation allows, we prepare for fight or flight: a cascade of hormones is produced, increasing heart and respiration rates, and making more oxygen available to the large muscles we need to fight or flee. If the situation seems so dire that fight or flight isn't possible, then another, phylogenetically older system[21] kicks in, and we freeze, essentially playing dead in hopes that the predator passes by.

What makes panic so effective as a survival skill is that we react not only to clear and present danger, but also to anything that reminds

---

[20] I use the term "panic" here not in the technical sense of panic disorder, but more generally as synonymous with "a lot of anxiety," with a connotation of particularly troublesome and compelling anxiety.

[21] Phylogenetically older means that this system developed at an earlier stage of evolution. Stephen Porges's Polyvagal Theory (2009) describes how different branches of the vagus nerve system regulate the fight-or-flight response (ventrovagal system) or freeze response (dorsovagal system), with the dorsovagal system developing earlier in evolution.

us of past danger. That's why we are so adept at learning from near misses: once burned, twice shy. And there's a clear survival advantage to reacting at the first sign of anything similar to a past danger, even if it turns out to be a false alarm. To overreact is uncomfortable and perhaps inconvenient, but to underreact could be deadly.

Therefore, we have evolved to panic too much rather than too little. Evolution errs on the side of caution when it comes to survival; our forebears were the people who knew how to panic, and we've inherited that ability.

Panic and Relationships

A funny thing happened on the way to becoming human: we developed language and abstract thought, to the extent that we can threaten or feel threatened just by speaking or hearing particular words. Moreover, we can sense a threat just by thinking of a potential danger, even when no actual external danger is present. Basically, we can worry ourselves into a panic.

Evolution didn't build this capability for worry from scratch; instead, it built on the mechanisms that were already there in earlier species. Whether we sense a potential attack from a predator or stew about a past disagreement with a spouse, the physiology of our anxiety response tends to be pretty much the same in kind, if not in degree. Our heart and respiration rates increase, and the chunks of cerebral cortex that deal with rational thought, foresight, and complex perspective tend to shut down. When we're freaking out, we can't think things through—as far as our brains and bodies are concerned, this is no time for a chat.

How does this affect relationships? For our species (not uniquely, but especially), the potential loss of a primary relationship feels dangerous, and our physiological response to that danger shuts down our capacity for rational thought (the better to fight you with, my dear). And at the level of the limbic system in the midbrain, the signs of danger—of the potential loss of the relationship—could be as simple as an important person rejecting you in a small way.

If we're important to each other, we're good at tuning in to each other's feelings—especially if we sense rejection. And that means that my panic can easily become your panic. As you experience my distress as a potential loss, your distress can ramp up, which then confirms my fears, and we're off and running. Worse, my fears about your reaction might not even be an accurate read of a particular situation—maybe you were just annoyed by something or someone else. But if I take your reaction personally, my panic will become your problem, and I'll produce just what I was fearing in the first place.

Fortunately, we're not exclusively governed by our limbic reactions. The tendency for the cerebral cortex to shut down when we feel threatened isn't all-or-nothing, and there are opportunities for other systems to moderate the effects of panic. Indeed, learning to make use of those other systems, through practice, is one way of understanding how therapy can help you.

Lowering Versus Tolerating Anxiety

Let's revisit the two golden gifts we talked about in Chapter 2. We need stability, which means we need to be able to lower or avoid anxiety, so as not to threaten our relationships with excessive panicking. Therefore, we steer clear of fear as much as we can. Since we find our partners' negative reactions unpleasant, and therefore anxiety-producing, we try to avoid triggering them.[22] This means that we learn to tolerate many of the differences we encounter, rather than threaten the relationship by making an issue of them. Couples who aren't able to calm themselves enough to deal with differences have a very hard time maintaining stable relationships (recall Tara and Trey). A lot of the techniques used in therapy, especially individual therapy, are about helping us calm ourselves.

But we also need intimacy, which means we must be able to tolerate the inevitable anxiety that comes with speaking honestly to

---

[22]If you don't find your partner's negative reactions unpleasant, perhaps that's because you aren't detecting your partner's distress. If you're not skilled at picking up those cues, which is one way of being neuroatypical (e.g., Asperger's Syndrome), working with a therapist with expertise in neuroatypicality can help you develop the skills you need to improve your relationship. If, on the other hand, you do detect your partner's negative reactions, but don't find them unpleasant—or worse, if you enjoy them—then you're a sociopath and shouldn't be in an intimate relationship. Of course, if that's you, you're very unlikely to be reading this book, so it probably isn't you!

someone important. Indeed, it's the very importance of the relationship that raises your anxiety, because being honest with your partner about something you object to or something you want risks opposition, rejection, or disconnection from your partner. Intimacy is scary with someone who matters. Many couples avoid the anxiety by suppressing objections, desires, or deep feelings so as not to threaten the stability of the relationship. That can work for a while—sometimes a long while. But couples who shut down intimacy are dying a slow death. They will find ways to break free; affairs are often how they do it.

Tolerating anxiety, not lowering or avoiding it, is a prerequisite for intimacy. That's because dealing with something important often requires us to raise our own, and our partner's, anxiety. Hence the tension between stability skills and intimacy skills. If I learn how to calm myself, I can keep my thinking brain functional enough to not run screaming from the room when something is amiss. But if I'm so afraid of the discomfort of anxiety that I try to avoid it altogether, I'll find that I also avoid bringing up difficult but important issues, thereby stifling intimacy.

If only we could eliminate anxiety, we could have both stability and intimacy with ease. After all, isn't it our anxiety, and our ability to stimulate it in our partners, that deprives us of both stability and intimacy?

Anxiety Is an Integral Part of Life

Life without anxiety would be meaningless. Lest you think me heartless, let me put that idea in perspective. My point isn't that anxiety itself is what gives life meaning. And when you're in the midst of extreme anxiety—in moments of panic—you'll want to do almost anything to stop it. Our capacity to panic has evolved for just that purpose: it signals us to drop everything else and do something—anything—to change our current situation.

But eliminating our capacity to panic also eliminates our capacity to care. Anxiety is how I respond when I sense something vital is in imminent danger. Of course, I'll feel anxiety when I'm under attack from a predator. But if I don't also feel anxiety when I sense that my spouse is angry with me, I won't act in ways to avoid that situation, which, from my spouse's point of view, makes me an inconsiderate jerk. To care about someone is, at least in part, to feel at risk when you think about losing the relationship.[23] Love entails anxiety.

More broadly, to love anything—be it a person, thing, abstract idea, or whatever—is to experience anxiety when you sense that it is at risk. Anxiety and its situational manifestations of guilt, shame, and grief are all indices of care. Without them we would be impervious to morality (guilt), cultural norms (shame), and deep attachment (grief). These are the characteristics that make us human and give us a sense of meaning. Anxiety isn't a bug of human evolution; it's a feature.

The admonition "Don't panic" in our seven-word formula doesn't mean that you shouldn't be *able* to panic. It's just a shorthand way of saying that you need, both individually and as a couple, to keep your (inevitable) anxiety within limits that allow for both stability and intimacy. And many couples learn those skills by encountering a particular kind of crisis in their relationship. Whether they manage to survive as a couple often depends on how they get through that crisis.

Reflections: Panic and Its Effects (Good and Bad)

1. Recall a few times when you were anticipating some event that caused you anxiety—say, when you were about to give a presentation, take an important exam, go for a job interview, go on a date, or bring up something serious with your partner. Undoubtedly, some events caused you more anxiety than others. How did your anxiety get in the way? What did you do to manage the anxiety so you could get through the event?

2. How has anxiety helped you? When you're preparing for a performance or presentation, too much anxiety can be disabling. But have you ever found that moderate anxiety can help keep you focused? Have you ever been grateful for anxiety that steered you away from something?

---

[23]This might explain why the Mother Teresas and Ghandis of the world often seem to have difficulty with close personal relationships. To devote yourself to everyone without regard to your own desires can mean that you don't feel particular kinship with the people closest to you.

CHAPTER 4

THE DEATH SPIRAL FOR PASSION

What Happened to the Spark?

Remember Deirdre and Patrick from Chapter 1? They had started out together as friends, then rapidly progressed to being passionate lovers before getting married and starting a life together.

Now, seventeen years into their marriage, the only intense connection they had on most days was mutual irritation. Dierdre was annoyed by pretty much everything Patrick did, and she bristled especially at his efforts to connect with her. Patrick alternated between frustration and despair: each time he would sense a potential softening from Dierdre, he would try to start a conversation or suggest an activity, only to be rejected yet again. In his frustration, Patrick would sometimes lash out verbally, which only reinforced Dierdre's irritation. Lately, despair was winning out.

Not surprisingly, their once lively sex life had become less and less active after Dierdre made it clear that she wasn't going to dutifully put out anymore (for example, on Patrick's birthday), and would only have sex if she really wanted to. Patrick, for his part, didn't want mercy sex either—he wanted Dierdre to desire him. Which, as of late, she didn't.

And it wasn't just that she wasn't "in the mood." Lots of people find that, when there's general good will between them and their partner, they are willing to make some effort to get in the mood, because they have a good time once they get going and they realize it's good for the relationship. No, for Dierdre, this was more about active hostility than a lack of interest or effort.

How did this happen? And why does this happen to so many couples?

There are, of course, many factors besides relationship issues that can affect someone's libido. A couple can have a deeply loving relationship, with all the hallmarks of stability and intimacy, and yet one or both members might still experience low libido. Hormone levels, other physiological conditions (such as an underlying illness, medications, and the like), and circumstantial factors (work stresses, financial worries) are often key. And it's not always obvious that those factors are at play, because human sex drive is complex, and the relational, physiological, and circumstantial causes interact. That's why it's important to consider multiple possibilities when you're dealing with issues of sexual desire. As with many other issues that are apt to come up in a therapist's office, sometimes a medical consultation is a crucial step in finding a solution.

But for many couples, the problem isn't low libido per se. Dierdre, for example, was convinced that she had as much libido as she ever had. The problem, she felt, wasn't that she lacked interest in sex; it was that she was constantly irritated by Patrick. For many other couples, the problem doesn't present itself as active hostility, but as a sort of ennui, a feeling that something that was once vital and vigorous has become boring and stale.

If it isn't a medical problem, and it isn't external stressors, then what's happening? How do couples who start out hot and spicy end up cold and bitter?

Oddly enough, it's not just because the novelty of a new lover wears off. It's true that we humans seek novelty in lots of ways, and sex with a new partner can be exciting simply because it's new. But I've seen lots of long-married couples experience bursts of sexual passion with each other when some crisis occurs—say, after one has had an affair, or even moved out. I don't in the slightest recommend having an affair or moving out to spice up your marriage, because that will probably end it. But those examples serve to illustrate that you don't need a new partner to have a renewed relationship, because it's not about switching partners.

And it's not just about the raging hormones of youth. While twenty-five-year-olds are usually capable of more sexual gymnastics or more frequent orgasms than their elders, the deepest expressions of intimacy, and even the most intense levels of sexual connection, come with maturity.[24]

So no, the real buzz-killer is not familiarity or lost youth. The real buzz-killer is anxiety—well, not really anxiety itself, but what we do to avoid anxiety.

Think about it. As we've discussed, you want intimacy, but you also want stability. In fact, once you've found what feels like intimacy— once you love someone and sense that they love you—one of your biggest fears is losing that feeling. It's terrifying, and it gets more frightening as you become more important to each other.

And that fear of loss, ironically, is what drives the death spiral that kills intimacy. Because as it turns out, that amazing person you fell in love with is actually different from you, and some of those differences are scary. He doesn't like the way she talks about his family. She doesn't like how his family talks about her. She doesn't like how he seems to flirt with everyone. He doesn't like how she gets distant from him when they're out together with other people. Neither one of them likes how the other spends money, or cleans too much or too little, or even sleeps. Or makes love. Or wants to make love. Or doesn't want to make love.

At first, it's easy enough to ignore the differences, just accept them, or even revel in them. But sooner or later you encounter differences you can't ignore, and can't just accept, either. You need to do something. So, you try to bring up how you felt when your partner talked to you that way or touched you in a way that was uncomfortable. Or, perhaps you've noticed your partner seems to be avoiding you, and you're worried about it. Or maybe you really, really want to try something in bed, but you don't know how your partner will react if you bring it up.

And that's the problem: you don't know how your partner will react when you bring it up. Maybe you've already experienced times when it went off the rails—when you ended up in a screaming fight,

---

[24]David Schnarch (2011) notes (p.162): "Your capacity for desire typically increases as you age. Some couples solve desire problems later in life that they simply couldn't handle when they were younger."

or a deep freeze. You get sensitized to each other's rising anxiety. The more important you are to each other, the more you tune in to each other's fears. And when you sense that your partner is getting upset, it upsets you, too.

Fire and Ice

What happens next depends on your particular style as a couple. Let me refer you to Robert Frost's poem, "Fire and Ice" (1920):

Some say the world will end in fire,
Some say in ice.
From what I've tasted of desire
I hold with those who favor fire.
But if it had to perish twice,
I think I know enough of hate
To say that for destruction ice
Is also great
And would suffice.

If your destruction style is fire, your relationship will turn into a war zone: Anything can set you off. You might have periods of truce, or even hot connection, but eventually your mutual reactivity will go nuclear. If it keeps on like that, you'll never be able to trust each other's good will.

If it's ice that kills your passion, you won't start a fight when you come across a scary difference. Instead, you'll gradually reduce what you're willing to risk with each other. You'll find yourself censoring what you might bring up to avoid triggering anxiety. You'll give up on any sort of sexual activity that risks anxiety and settle on routines you're both comfortable with, which reduces your love-making repertoire to the dreary and predictable, which might turn into nothing at all. You'll keep more and more of yourself hidden, at least from your partner. You'll shut down more and more of yourself for the sake of peace. You'll feel like you're carrying around a heavy weight at home. Some people in this situation succumb to the lure of an affair—it's so compelling when you can actually be yourself with someone who seems to want you as you are.

Either way, whether it's by fire or by ice—or by some combination of the two—if left unchecked, this destruction will leave you feeling alone, frustrated, and miserable.

That, more or less, is what happened with Patrick and Dierdre. What started as minor differences, small perceived slights, and mini disappointments morphed with time into a grand narrative of mutual mistrust, as their assumptions of good will eroded with each new instance of misunderstanding and recrimination. Their style, as with many couples, had elements of both fire and ice: their frequent episodes of disconnection would send them into a freeze-thaw cycle, occasionally punctuated by an eruption of anger when one or the other couldn't contain their hurt.

Becoming Aware of Assumptions

This cycle was compounded for Dierdre when she realized that she had been putting up with a lot from Patrick, simply because she assumed that she had to.

For example, in the past couple years, she realized that she had often been having sex with Patrick even when she didn't particularly want to, just because she's his wife and wives are supposed to do that. She knew perfectly well that having sex should always be a consensual activity for both parties. However, the cultural norms[25] that she had absorbed operate unconsciously, so it often didn't occur to her that she had a genuine choice.

And, of course, Patrick's assumptions based on those same norms rendered him unaware that he was pressuring her, even though, if asked, he would agree that they should have sex only if they both sincerely wanted it. So, he would sometimes—not often, but often enough—react to her "not tonight" as a personal affront and respond coldly, effectively punishing her for her honesty.

This reflected two unconscious assumptions on Patrick's part. The first was that if he wants sex, his wife is supposed to provide it willingly, if not enthusiastically. This assumption was hard for him to recognize,

---

[25]These cultural norms can be summarized in the word "patriarchy," referring to a host of assumptions and power relations that systematically privilege men and disempower women.

because if he had been asked about it, he would have sincerely denied having that view. He didn't want to think of himself as that kind of man, and he was genuinely unaware of his attitude. But if some part of him didn't feel that way, he wouldn't have responded to his wife with coldness when she declined sex. If he truly saw her having sex with him as her choice rather than her duty, he might be disappointed when she turned him down, but he wouldn't try to make her feel bad, as if she had failed in an obligation.[26]

The second assumption was that if she disappoints him, some desire to punish her is a direct result of what she did. To many men (and women, for that matter), this seems so obvious as to be tautological: If you're hurt by someone, aren't you apt to get angry? And if you're angry, don't you want to punish the one who hurt you? But curiously, those same men often respond very differently when they are disappointed by someone whose power they respect, such as a boss or a business client who can fire them. The point isn't that we don't get angry at bosses. Of course we do—but when we do, we're generally very careful about how we express it, lest we suffer the consequences. Getting mouthy with a boss who pissed you off seems like adolescent behavior, precisely because they have power over you.[27] Conversely, if I'm trying to punish someone for their behavior (be it with fire or ice), I'm assuming that I have the power, and implicitly the right, to control their behavior. Patrick wouldn't have said that was his intention, but his actions demonstrate that part of him felt that way.

Patrick was oblivious to his own part in this cycle. From his perspective, he wasn't pressuring her for sex or punishing her for withholding it; rather, he was just responding naturally to her seemingly constant rejection. Since he loved Dierdre and saw himself as a respectful and considerate man, he was mystified by her growing resentment of him, and could only conclude that she was hypersensitive or otherwise messed up emotionally. The more she pushed him away, the more he considered his own angry reactions as natural consequences of her hostility, rather than contributing factors

---

[26]Marital rape did not become illegal in all of the United States until 1993. The assumption that a woman's consent to marriage provides perpetual consent to sex any time the husband wants it is deeply embedded.

[27]Someone who gets out of line with a boss is apt to be stigmatized as needing "anger management."

to their mutual pain. In other words, he simply "knew" that she's the one who needed fixing, not he.

That conclusion itself fits well with the cultural messages that men are generally sane, logical, sensible, and strong, while women are prone to being irrational, emotional, erratic, and weak. Patrick viewed his own anger as understandable, and Dierdre's anger as inexplicable. There must be something wrong with her. His presence in couples therapy was testimony to his sincere willingness to help—that is, to help her get over it.

A lot of women in this kind of situation blame themselves as much as their husbands blame them, and then those women become depressed. (Recall Sharon from Chapter 1, who became suicidal.) Fortunately for Dierdre, she refused to accept the idea that her resentment and irritability reflected something fundamentally wrong with her. She was angry, not depressed. As she began to assert her own dignity and autonomy, she became increasingly aware of how much she had been hurt by Patrick over the decades.

This might have led Dierdre to the conclusion that Patrick is hopelessly mean-spirited, or pushed her to end the marriage in hopes of finding another man who would treat her with respect and kindness. She might have concluded that marriage is inherently degrading for women, given the pervasiveness of the attitude she was dealing with. Patrick might have concluded that Dierdre was so deeply and irrevocably contemptuous of him and that staying with her was unbearable.

But neither of them had reached those conclusions. They were deeply hurt, not only by what they each had experienced from the other, but also by guilt from knowing the pain they each had caused. What brought them to my office were remnants of hope—a hope that the love and trust they once felt for each other could be revived. For that to happen, they would both need to tolerate the anxiety of hearing each other speak honestly—that is, the anxiety of intimate engagement. To tolerate that anxiety without descending into panic was the challenge they faced.

That work is inherently difficult for couples who have been trapped in the death spiral of passion for years. They must be willing and able to risk the very uncertainty that they had been avoiding in their effort to maintain stability.

Taking that risk involves not only honesty with each other, but honesty with yourself, which is much harder. To let yourself hear the cacophony of voices within—to let yourself know what you know—without completely losing perspective is not easy.[28] And it's particularly difficult to let yourself know what you know when some of that information is so terrifying that you dissolve into panic just at its very mention.

Simply put, in order to do the work of tolerating intimacy, you need to heal from trauma.

Reflections:
The Death Spiral for Passion

1. Have you experienced the death spiral we've talked about in this chapter? Think about relationships you've had, past or present, which started out passionate but cooled over time. Can you recall occasions when you stopped yourself from discussing something with your partner because you were too anxious? Might your partner have done the same sometimes? What effects did those occasions have on intimacy in the relationship?

2. Think of a time when you were anxious about bringing something up with your partner, but did so anyway. How did you manage to tolerate the anxiety? How did the conversation go? What effect did it have on intimacy?

---

[28]Richard Schwartz (1995) and his colleagues have developed the Internal Family Systems (IFS) approach to therapy. IFS starts from the premise that we all have multiple parts to our personalities, each of which is valid and important, even though they may be causing dysfunction. The techniques of IFS therapy are designed to help you access your true Self, your spiritual core, inviting it to engage with those parts in a spirit of curiosity and acceptance in order to heal and harmonize them.

I've found this idea helpful for many clients, especially for helping them recognize the conflicting desires and fears of different parts. You're not crazy to be stuck—it's just that different parts of you want or fear opposite things, for valid reasons. When you help those parts with their fears, you can find ways of harmonizing them, and then you're not stuck anymore. I'm not using IFS terminology in this book, but I think many of the concepts here are compatible with IFS ideas.

CHAPTER 5

TRAUMA AND RELATIONSHIPS

What Is Trauma?

The word "trauma" has a more general meaning in medical settings, but I'm talking about trauma as it is used in psychotherapy: an experience that hurt you emotionally or psychologically, and continues to hurt you afterward—perhaps even long afterward.

According to the Center for Integrated Health Solutions of the National Council for Behavioral Health, "In the United States 61 percent of men and 50 percent of women report exposure to at least one lifetime traumatic event, and 90 percent of clients in public behavioral health care settings have experienced trauma" (SAMHSA - HRSA, 2019). Of course, these statistics depend on how the researchers define and count traumatic events.[29] But the point is that experiencing trauma at some time in our lives isn't rare; it's the norm.

Whether or not we call it trauma, everyone gets hurt sometimes, in small ways or big ones. What makes such an event traumatic (for our purposes) is if your body continues to react to it as an emergency— in other words, you enter a state of panic—even when the event is no longer happening.

---

[29]I suspect that the finding that more men than women reported trauma in the CIHS study has to do not only with the definitions they're using, but also with cultural trends in what people think of as traumatic. Since the explosion of public discussion around the #MeToo movement in 2017, I've heard from many women about experiences of sexual violations many years before that they are only now recognizing as having had traumatic effects.

We all know what an emergency feels like. We'd better know, since it's a crucial survival mechanism.

As we discussed in Chapter 3, when we perceive an immediate, dangerous threat, our brains and bodies prepare us to fight an attacker, run away, or in the most terrifying situations, freeze up completely. Fight, flight, or freeze: these are abilities that we share with other mammals and even reptiles.

The fight or flight response requires that lots of oxygen be sent to the big muscles, so our heart and respiration rates increase. Our pupils dilate, and both vision and hearing change to become more focused and less distracted by anything peripheral. Any parts that are unnecessary for the emergency lose blood flow. We sweat to provide cooling from the heat that will be generated by the large movements involved in our fighting or fleeing.

That's why your heart pounds, your breathing speeds up, you sweat, you feel tingly, and you get tunnel vision. Your body is getting ready to fight or flee.

Fight or flight is what you do when you perceive a potential way out. Freeze is what you do in a desperate attempt to survive when you see no way out. This can happen when you perceive the imminent danger as inescapable. You can also freeze when something so horrible has occurred that you simply can't accept it, because it's too overwhelming. In a lot of ways, the freeze response is the opposite of fight or flight: Instead of preparing for large muscle movements, the body shuts down. Muscles freeze or lose tone completely—essentially, you play dead, which might result in a potential predator moving on. It's why people sometimes collapse when confronted with horrendous news or after seeing a horrendous sight.

Whether it's the fight-or-flight response or the freeze response, the calm, rational-thinking parts of the brain go offline. When the tiger is at the door of your cave, there's no time to think calmly about your options. That's why when you're in a panic, you *can't* think clearly.

It's not just our rational thinking that shuts down. We also know that in humans, the perception of a serious threat releases a cascade of hormones that, among other things, affect the part of the brain that stores conscious memories. So if you've been through a traumatic event, it's very possible you don't consciously remember the worst moments of it. Or, you may have clear memories of certain parts, but little or no memory of others.[30]

Alternatively, you might remember the events, but not the feelings associated with them—in effect, you prevent conscious awareness of the parts that might otherwise be intolerable. This is also a survival mechanism called dissociation. In extreme circumstances—particularly those involving frequent and severe trauma during early childhood—a person might dissociate to such an extent that they form distinct identities. This phenomenon is called Dissociative Identity Disorder (DID). A person with DID might manifest many different personalities and switch from one to another without knowing it. Though DID can cause chaos in a person's life and relationships, it's not a brain malfunction; rather, it's an adaptation to horrendous circumstances. We've adopted the ability to dissociate because we need it—sometimes we need to stop ourselves from experiencing something consciously, lest we be so overwhelmed that we can't function at all.

But when you've gone through a traumatic event, even if you don't remember it consciously, your brain and body are changed by it: you have learned to react to anything that might remind you, even unconsciously, of the event. This is another survival mechanism: we learn very quickly to go into emergency mode if we sense even a hint of a past trauma. This happens very quickly, much faster than our conscious can process. It's a vital skill. If we didn't learn in that way, we'd never have survived as a species. Our bodies learn to react when something remotely similar happens, even if it isn't actually dangerous. In effect, we become hyper-alert to danger.

We talked in Chapter 3 about how our tendency to panic affects our relationships. First, recall that your reactions to seemingly small slights in an important relationship are built on the same mechanism that protects you from predators: in some ways, you can feel like you're about to be eaten when your spouse is annoyed with you. Add to that your ability to

---

[30]Dr. Christine Blasey Ford's testimony in the Kavanagh Supreme Court confirmation hearings of 2018 served to educate the public on this phenomenon, both in terms of her own experience and her expertise in the neuroscience involved.

think symbolically and imagine the future, which means you're capable of worrying yourself into a panic. The more important a relationship becomes, the more you're apt to panic when you even imagine something threatening it, because your fear of its loss triggers the same kind of responses you feel when you're under attack from a predator.

As we discussed in Chapter 4, one of the prerequisites for a passionate relationship is the ability to tolerate the anxiety of emotional honesty with yourself and your partner. And that's where the effects of trauma become particularly acute. More precisely, that's where the effects of *unhealed* trauma become particularly acute.

Healed and Unhealed Trauma

Note that our practical definition of trauma above doesn't just refer to some experience that hurts you; rather, a key part of the definition is that the experience *continues* to hurt you, often long after the event occurred. This trauma is unhealed to the extent that a reminder of the event, even unconsciously, is still causing you to click into emergency mode. Conversely, if a reminder of the event *doesn't* result in an emergency response, then the trauma is healed.

Now most of the time, when you've been through a traumatic event, you do eventually heal psychologically. How do you know you've healed? When you've healed emotionally from a hurt, it means that when you think or talk about it, you experience it as a memory. It might be a sad memory, a scary memory, an embarrassing memory, or even a tragic one, but whatever emotions come with it, it's still a memory. It happened in the past—it's not happening to you now. You've been through it, and you came out the other side. You can decide to keep thinking about it or not. You can see the grays, as well as the black and white. You might shed a tear, but you won't freak out.

That's what it feels like when you've healed: it's no longer an emergency. However bad the event was at the time, it's no longer having a traumatic effect.

How do you know if you haven't healed from a hurt? Or, to put it another way, how do you know if the hurt is still having a traumatic effect? You haven't healed if the memory isn't just a memory. Instead, it still feels like an immediate, present emergency, and your body responds accordingly with a fight, flight, or freeze response.

This response to an unhealed trauma is qualitatively different from the emotions you might experience when you remember a healed one. An unhealed trauma response feels immediately dangerous. In extreme cases, called flashbacks, you can feel like the original trauma is happening to you again in the present. The response happens so quickly that you might not have any idea of what triggered it. Some people have trauma responses involving sudden loss of bowel or bladder control, loss of consciousness, or extreme rage. More commonly, a trauma response can result in a disabling panic attack.

By contrast, when you're having an emotional response to a healed memory, you remain aware that you're in the present, and you recognize your emotions as a response to the memory—in other words, you can form a coherent understanding of how you're feeling.[31] You might be bothered, but you're not in a panic.

The brain processes that produce trauma responses are much faster than those that underlie consciousness. More simply, when something reminds your brain of the trauma, your body responds before you are even aware of it. If your response is fast enough, you might not even realize what triggered the response; all you know is that your body has gone into panic mode for no apparent reason. And even if you do know what triggered the response, your panic reactions are well under way before you can intervene consciously.

If you've experienced this, you know how disturbing and disruptive it can be. It's scary and disorienting; you start to doubt your sanity. And if you don't know what triggered it, you become hyper-alert to possible signs that you're panicking, which just makes you more likely to panic. It's a nasty cycle. It's even nastier if you've experienced repeated trauma over a long period of time, because your body becomes so primed to detect possible danger that your reactions become part of the problem.

Unhealed trauma can make a mess of your life, especially when the trauma stemmed from experiences in important relationships, because there are so many parallels you can draw between your current relationship and earlier ones. To take an obvious example, if you've been sexually

---

[31]Your understanding of your emotional response to a memory might not always be objectively accurate; for example, you might be reminded of something your father did, and find yourself annoyed at your husband or therapist. Psychodynamic therapists refer to this as transference.

traumatized in the past, sex with someone in the present—even when it's entirely consensual and in a loving context—can be fraught with triggers, consciously or unconsciously, that remind you of the trauma and send your body into emergency mode. And if your partner feels threatened by your emergency response, and responds in kind, you both end up further sensitized, and the pattern becomes all the more likely in the future.

The way out of this, of course, is to heal from the trauma. Fortunately, there's help available. Over the past couple of decades, the field of therapy has made enormous progress in learning how to help people heal from trauma.

Healing from Trauma

How does healing from trauma happen? And how can we set up the right conditions to encourage that healing?

As I previously mentioned, after experiencing a traumatic event, more often than not, we heal. After some period of time, when we are reminded of the event, consciously or unconsciously, we stay on an even keel emotionally. It's not an emergency. If we're conscious of it, we experience it as a memory, not as a present danger.

How do our bodies and minds manage to recover from trauma on their own? After all, isn't that hyper-alert reaction that we develop after a traumatic event an important survival mechanism? How do we manage to unlearn it over time?

To understand how we heal is to understand how we learn anything new. Many years ago, the neuroscientist Donald Hebb described a theory of what goes on in our brains when we learn: neurons that fire together wire together.[32] Keep firing the same brain circuits at the same time, and pretty soon they turn into one circuit—all you have to do is trigger one part of it, and the whole thing fires automatically.

Look at a toddler learning to walk, or a musician practicing a difficult passage, and you'll see this principle in action. At first, a skill starts out as a series of separate parts, lurching from one part to another. But after some repetition, it turns into a single, coordinated skill. The separate circuits have become one—what fires together, wires together.

---

[32]Paraphrased from Hebb (1949).

This happens at an amazing rate in young children, but it also happens to some extent in adults of any age. Turns out you *can* teach an old dog new tricks. It's what neuroscientists call "neuroplasticity."

What has to wire together to heal a trauma? What circuits do you need to fire together to produce healing? Well, healing is when you can remember the event, and still feel sufficiently safe that your body doesn't go into emergency mode. So those are the circuits that need to fire together repeatedly: you need to pair the memory of the event with the feeling of sufficient safety. If you experience the memory and still feel basically safe, your brain and body will learn that it's safe to experience the memory. That's how you heal.

And, as I said, usually you do heal. Usually you have enough experience of remembering the trauma and at the same time feeling safe, that the two wire together: you learn to feel safe when you remember the trauma.

Note that you don't have to feel completely at ease; you just have to feel safe enough that you're not panicking. Indeed, tolerating some amount of anxiety is necessary for healing, just as it's necessary for intimacy in a relationship. The key is being able to accept that a little anxiety is not in itself an emergency.

You can get healing experiences in all sorts of ways. Maybe you talk about the events with caring friends or loved ones—notice how that pairs the experience of memory with safety. Or maybe you're just able to calm yourself when you think of it. Over time, you have enough experiences of remembering the event and simultaneously feeling safe that you're healed: the experience has become a memory, and the memory isn't an emergency.

But, as you know, sometimes you don't heal from trauma on your own. Why is that? Why do some traumatic events continue to cause an emergency response, sometimes for decades?

Recall what helps you heal, and apply that logic in reverse. If you're not able to experience the memory and still feel sufficiently safe, the memory will continue to produce an emergency response—you'll keep panicking when the memory is triggered.

This is why, sometimes, talking about an experience doesn't help. If talking about it triggers reactions that are so upsetting that you can't simultaneously feel safe, then talking about it makes it worse, not better. It's what we refer to as re-traumatizing. This often happens to children, as well as adults, who are sexually abused and not believed (or worse, punished) by the people they rely on to care for them. Many adult survivors have told me that the reaction from the people they told was a worse trauma, in terms of long-lasting effects, than the sexual abuse itself.

Another reason why you might not be able to heal on your own is if you can't feel safe at all. If you grew up feeling unsafe, or are living in an abusive situation, you might have a hard time feeling safe at any time.

And sometimes, even if you can feel safe, and you can talk about a traumatic event without panicking, you still might not heal. That's because of another survival mechanism: the ability to dissociate, which means to block some or all of the experience from awareness. Dissociation helps you cope day-to-day, but it leaves the trauma unhealed. It's also why traditional talk therapy is often limited in its ability to fully heal trauma. If you're essentially talking around the problem, it doesn't do much good.

Psychoactive substances such as alcohol, marijuana, cocaine, and opiates are also effective ways of dissociating, which (perhaps) is why people with unhealed trauma are particularly prone to addiction. Since healing requires you to be emotionally present (albeit in a safe way), chronic substance use prevents healing. Co-occurring unhealed trauma and addiction can be particularly difficult to treat, because the two conditions support each other: the unhealed trauma ramps up the anxiety that drives the addiction, and the addiction prevents effective healing of the trauma.

So what can you do? As I noted earlier, since researchers have come to understand what's happening when you experience unhealed trauma, therapeutic approaches have been developed that can better aid the healing process. Examples of these approaches include (among others): Eye Movement Desensitization and Reprocessing (EMDR Institute, Inc., 2019), Prolonged Exposure (APA, 2019), and Stress Inoculation Therapy (Mills, H., Reiss, N. & Dombeck, M., 2019). Researchers have also found that some of these techniques can be used in combination with treatments for addiction, so that the mutually reinforcing cycle of trauma and addiction can be dismantled (National Center for PTSD, 2019).

While the various approaches differ in theory and in practice, they can each provide the necessary conditions for healing trauma by helping you feel sufficiently safe, even when the trauma circuits are triggered. By firing the neurons that encode the memory of the trauma (usually by inviting you to remember the event), and firing the neurons that encode the feeling of safety, the treatment encourages your brain to wire those sets of neurons together. You learn to feel safe even when you're reminded of the traumatic event. You experience it as a memory, not an emergency.

Of course, any therapeutic approach is valuable only to the extent that you are willing and able to make use of it. Ultimately, reaching out for help is an act of courage. You can't know for sure if it will help, or if you can tolerate what it takes to heal, until you actually experience it. But doing the work of healing with commitment and resolve is a vital step toward being able to pull yourself together when it matters most.

Denial Doesn't Help

If you're concerned about the effects of trauma on a relationship, you want the situation to get better. If you're the one with unhealed trauma, you want to heal; and if you're in a relationship with someone who has unhealed trauma, you want to help them heal. Of course, you might be in both of those roles.

We've been talking about how unhealed trauma affects us, and what conditions are needed to heal. But there is a common reaction to unhealed trauma that certainly does *not* help—common enough that it's worth discussing.

That unhelpful reaction is denial. Denial of the problem doesn't make it go away. Now, it's quite possible that even major events such as rape, assault, or near-fatal accidents have happened to you, and you've been able to heal. People can and do heal from horrendous experiences on their own—just because you've been badly hurt doesn't mean you're still traumatized. That's not denial, it's healing.

But if you're still reacting with panic to certain situations that don't represent acute danger in themselves—for example, if you dissociate when you're having consensual sex, or panic when you see a television program that references a similar traumatic event—then the unhealed trauma is interfering with your life, and you need to get appropriate treatment. You might be trying to ignore the problem by avoiding the things that trigger you, consciously or not. But that strategy nearly always fails, for two reasons: first, your need to avoid triggers is apt to ruin relationships you care about (to cite an obvious example, avoiding sex because it causes panic isn't usually great for a couple); and second, avoiding triggers deprives you of the experiences you need to heal, as we discussed previously.

Denial is also a counterproductive strategy if you're trying to help a loved one who has experienced trauma. As I noted earlier, I've been told by many survivors that the lack of support from those closest to them caused even more traumatic effects than the original abuse. Unfortunately, this pattern can get replicated when a survivor's trauma symptoms surface long after the original event—triggered, say, by a survivor's child reaching the age at which the survivor was abused, news stories about similar events, or other circumstantial similarities that arise. The attempts by significant others to make the survivor "snap out of it" just reinforce the cycle. And even worse, out-and-out denial of the survivor's experience constitutes a new trauma.[33]

If you're dealing with unhealed trauma, denial won't help you heal. You may find ways to heal without formal treatment, or you may need to seek help from a competent therapist. But either way, the work is yours to do.

Even when you've healed—indeed, even if you've been fortunate enough not to have experienced major traumatic events in the first place—you need to develop the skills that allow you to calm yourself when you're able to, without dissolving into panic. In other words, you must learn to get hold of yourself in order to tolerate the inevitable anxiety that arises in intimate relationships.

---

[33]Whatever you may believe about the fallibility of memory (of course it's fallible), a person who was in fact abused and then experiences denial of their abuse has been doubly injured.

Reflections: Trauma and Relationships

1. Think of a traumatic event in your life from which you've healed. What experiences and what people helped you heal? What did you learn from the experience of healing, perhaps about your own resilience?

2. If you're affected by unhealed trauma, what are you doing to help yourself heal?

3. If you're in a relationship with a partner who is affected by unhealed trauma, how have you tried to help? Have you been less than helpful sometimes? What have you learned about the effects of unhealed trauma that might help you in the relationship?

CHAPTER 6

GETTING HOLD OF YOURSELF

We All Get Anxious Sometimes

We've already discussed the importance of anxiety as a survival mechanism, and even the role of anxiety in making life meaningful. What you care about, you get anxious about; and if you don't get anxious about something, you don't really care about it. They're two sides of the same coin. Can you imagine caring about something, but not experiencing anxiety if that something is threatened? Anxiety is baked into the very concept of caring.

It follows, then, that the more you care about someone, the more prone you are to anxiety over potential disturbances in that relationship.

How a couple handles this inevitable anxiety is an indicator of how stable the relationship is, as well as how well the relationship can sustain intimate connection. When a couple is thrown into panic by differences (recall Tara and Trey), or avoids the anxiety of differences by shutting down intimacy (Doris and Ken), the relationship will eventually hit a crisis. When a couple can learn to calm themselves and tolerate the anxiety that comes with honesty, they can sustain both stability and intimacy.

The key to sustaining stability and intimacy is being able to get hold of yourself: that is, to be able to calm yourself down when you can, and tolerate anxiety for the sake of intimacy without dissolving into panic. I like the metaphor "get hold of yourself" because it suggests that you do for yourself what parents do for young children when they are scared: they hold them. To get hold of yourself is to reassure and comfort yourself, to give yourself a hug when you most need it, and to remind yourself, as a parent might, that you need to behave appropriately even when you're upset.

Getting Out of Sync

One of the graphs in John Gottman's book *Principia Amoris* (2015) plots a measure of a married couple's emotionality over fifteen minutes as they discuss a disagreement. The two lines (one each for the husband and wife) are reminiscent of the lovely synchronization we see in an ice dancer's performance: as one goes up or down, so goes the other. Gottman followed many such couples for years, bringing them back to his lab periodically to assess how they're doing in their marriage. What would you predict for this couple's future?

As Gottman pointed out, a marriage with that sort of graph is headed for failure. They were so well synchronized in their emotional reactions that one partner's anxiety triggered the other's, and their mutual reactivity spiraled into panic. Note that they were having a disagreement, not having sex. Their emotional measures were primarily indices of anger and frustration, not pleasurable excitement.

Mutual reactivity—being in sync with your significant other—can be lovely when your partner matches your joy and passion in intimate connection (sexually or otherwise).[34] But when you match your partner's anxiety, which in turn drives up your partner's anxiety even more, you've created a recipe for disaster. Which is to say, you need to learn to get hold of yourself, even—especially—when your partner is having a hard time doing so themselves.

One of the most important skills you must learn in order to get hold of yourself is the ability to not panic when you get out of sync with your partner. In this context, getting out of sync means managing your own anxiety while still being open to connection, even if your partner's anxiety is spiking.

---

[34]And even then, you need to be able to tolerate your fundamental separateness from your partner. As Esther Perel (2006) notes (p.60), "Our ability to tolerate our separateness—and the fundamental insecurity it engenders—is a precondition for maintaining interest and desire in a relationship."

How do you do learn to get hold of yourself if you're not already good at it? What can you work on?

We've already discussed (in Chapter 5) the effects of unhealed trauma on a relationship. When part of your brain goes offline thanks to a reminder of an unhealed trauma, it's nearly impossible to get hold of yourself. One thing you can do is get the help you need in order to heal that trauma.

But unhealed trauma is not the only source of panicky reactivity. Even if you've been spared major trauma, you may find that getting hold of yourself during a conflict with your partner is challenging.

Discovering Your Hidden Assumptions

If you accidentally step on your partner's toe—and I mean this literally, physically stepping on your partner's actual toe—and your partner screams in pain, you may find their reaction unpleasant, but you (most likely) will consider their reaction understandable. And if you're the one whose toe got stepped on, and *you* scream in pain, you (most likely) will consider your own reaction understandable. Screaming in pain is a kind of bodily panic, just what evolution calls for when you get stepped on. Evidently, our ancestors who did so survived better than those who didn't, presumably because they got out from being stepped on more quickly.

That's why you generally feel entitled to holler "ouch" when someone steps on your toe, and you give that same right to others when you step on theirs. As such, you don't question someone's motives or sanity if they holler "ouch" when their toe gets stepped on.

There are circumstances, of course, in which you wouldn't holler "ouch" when your toe gets stepped on (and I still mean that literally), because it would expose you to greater danger or shame. Someone hiding from an active shooter, or (for a less dire example) someone acting in a play, would suppress their instinct to holler if their toe gets stepped on. That you *can* suppress the instinct to holler in certain circumstances is a key insight: it means that hollering isn't an inevitable consequence of getting stepped on. How you evaluate the situation (consciously or unconsciously) plays a major role.

You also might not holler when your toe gets stepped on simply because you don't experience it as pain. If you're playing, or competing in a sport, you might not experience a foot stomp as something that requires a reaction. Again, how you evaluate the situation holistically is central to how you react.

That perception of hollering as a right depends on your view of the circumstances. But in most day-to-day situations, you accord that right to yourself and others when it comes to toes getting stepped on.

In your relationship, if you suppress your instinct to holler "ouch" when your partner steps on your toe because you have a well-founded fear of their reaction, your relationship is abusive.[35] Recognizing that you are entitled to holler "ouch" in appropriate circumstances is a step toward escaping that abuse.

On the other hand, if you react to your partner's accidental stomp by flying into a rage and attacking them physically or emotionally, you've left the domain of the acceptable. You're entitled to react, but not *over*react. Of course, what constitutes overreaction is based on cultural and familial norms; what's acceptable in one family may be unacceptable in another, and the rules (explicit or implicit) are often based on your gender and your position in the family.[36] But there's generally some sort of observable limit that you violate at your own peril. Just because you're programmed to panic when your foot gets stepped on doesn't mean that you can't moderate your reaction.

Obviously, most conflicts between couples aren't about stepping on each other's toes literally, but metaphorically. If you're with someone long enough, you're going to impinge on each other sometimes, physically or emotionally. And, just like being literally stepped on, how you experience your partner's actions depends on much more than what is said or done; it depends on what you think they are entitled to do, and how you react depends on what you think *you're* entitled to do.

We already described an example of this in Chapter 4, when

---

[35] I said "well-founded" fear because you might fear your partner's reaction based on past trauma involving someone else, rather than anything your current partner has done. If so, you need to work on healing from the trauma, because your current relationship won't work if you don't feel entitled to say "ouch" when necessary.

[36] I'm not saying the rules *should be* based on gender or family position, but rather that in practice they are. For an often-cited example, men's anger and women's anger in similar situations tend to be judged quite differently in terms of entitlement, with important effects on how people are treated when they get angry.

we talked about the assumptions Dierdre and Patrick were making without being fully aware of them. For years, Dierdre didn't feel she was allowed to deny Patrick sex, and Patrick felt entitled to punish her with coldness if she did. Neither of them would have agreed consciously with the assumptions they were enacting, but they were enacting them nonetheless. It was only when Dierdre started questioning her assumption and recognizing her right to deny unwanted sex that she was able to change her behavior, and thereby challenge Patrick's assumption.

Getting hold of yourself when you and your partner get out of sync—that key skill that prevents a couple from spiraling out of control when one or the other gets upset—requires checking your sense of who is entitled to what. And that sense is based on the assumptions you're making about the situation, many of which operate unconsciously.

If you interpret your partner's actions or reactions as understandable for someone of good will—that is, if you consider them entitled to those actions (in a positive, not pejorative sense)—you're likely to respond in a way that conveys good will yourself. Conversely, if you consider your partner's actions to be out of bounds, you're likely to respond in a way that conveys some sort of hostility, be it disapproval, defensiveness, trivialization, or pathologizing. Patrick's initial reactions to Dierdre's newfound entitlement included all of those, based partly on notions about what wives are supposed to do in a marriage, and partly on ideas about women's anger. These notions also led him to see Dierdre's behavior as indicative of mental illness. But it was his willingness to examine those assumptions that allowed him to participate in their couples therapy as a full partner, which in turn offered Dierdre some hope that they could come to an understanding.

What about your sense of entitlement to your own actions and reactions? If your response to a perceived slight from your partner is based on an assumption of your partner's good will, you might say "ouch" and raise an objection, but you won't go on the attack. If you do, you're (apparently) not assuming good will, unless you feel entitled to attack someone over an inadvertent mistake.[37]

---

[37]If that's you, you're a bully. As I noted earlier about sociopaths, if you're that kind of bully, you're probably not reading this book. More likely, if you find yourself attacking, there's some part of you that doubts your partner's good will.

The more difficult scenario is when you *do* doubt your partner's good will, justifiably—that is, you can tell they're angry at you, and they aren't particularly concerned with how you feel about it in the moment.

That's when getting hold of yourself is the most challenging, and also the most crucial. If you feel entitled to respond to your partner's hostility with your own hostility, you'll likely escalate the situation, because your hostility will simply justify that of your partner. The escalation will continue until one or both of you recognize that you've stepped out of bounds—that no matter what the other is doing, you're no longer entitled to the reaction you've been having. By then, you might have (jointly or individually) caused serious injury to the relationship.

But when you maintain a sense of responsibility for your reactions even in the face of hostility—which is what getting hold of yourself means—then you will tend to elicit calmer responses from your partner. If not, at least you won't be contributing more anxiety to the situation.

How can you stay in control even in the face of your partner's hostility? Paradoxically, you can do so if you accept that occasional anger (within bounds) is normal for both of you. If you don't panic when your partner is angry with you, you'll tend to respond with care and curiosity, rather than with more anger. In a relationship that's generally pleasant, you'll view moments of anger as worthy of concern, so you'll take your partner's complaints seriously.

Similarly, if you feel entitled to express your own occasional anger without panicking, you'll be more likely to keep your expression within bounds that are also acceptable to your partner. Thus, your partner will be more likely to respond in a way that lets you express your feelings. In this way, you'll be able to maintain responsibility for how you express yourself, even if your partner's reaction gets out of bounds.

Character, Guilt, and Shame

I've been discussing the ability to get hold of yourself even when your partner can't as a skill you can develop. Like any skill, you develop it with a combination of understanding and practice. As I just described, an important part of developing that skill is becoming aware of your sense of entitlement, and when you should and shouldn't question it.

Viewed merely as a skill, the idea of getting hold of yourself is similar to the idea of anger management, a topic on which you can find all sorts of advice, approaches, and treatments. If your anger gets out of bounds, you need to contain it and assume responsibility. The techniques of anger management are essentially about learning to control your behavior under stress. I don't want to minimize the value of those techniques.

But I want to invoke another way of looking at the concept of getting hold of yourself, not just as a behavioral skill to help relationships work better.

What if getting hold of yourself represents a fundamental commitment to something bigger—bigger than yourself, bigger than your partner, and even bigger than your relationship? What if you were to view getting hold of yourself not merely as instrumental to a happier relationship, but as part of who you are in the world?

I often hear people say, in describing their own panicked behavior when they are at odds with their partners, something like, "I become someone I don't want to be." That's what I'm referring to. When you say something like that, it's a statement of values, of personal ethics. It's not just observing how your behavior makes the situation with your partner worse; it's recognizing that you've failed in your commitment to being a better person. To use the Yiddish term, you're not being a *mensch*. It's not just about situational tactics—it's about personal identity.

If you feel yourself becoming someone you don't want to be, you must have some idea of who you *do* want to be—in other words, you know a *mensch* when you see one. You have a moral compass, even if all it tells you is that some actions are wrong. Getting hold of yourself in this sense means that you're guided by that moral compass, even when it's difficult.

You need a moral compass precisely because your impulses often push you in the opposite direction. Asking yourself "What's the right thing to do?" is very different from asking yourself "What do I feel like doing?" It's also different from asking "What will get me what I want in this situation?" You might hope those questions lead to the same result, but they often don't.

As we discussed in Chapter 2, doing the right thing even when you don't feel like it, and even when you aren't sure it will get you what you want, are hallmarks of character. To act as the person you want to be, even in conflict—to be a *mensch*—is to embody good character.

Notice that being of good character implies that you're guided by principles outside yourself, because you recognize that your own feelings aren't always a reliable guide to what's right. Of course, you're still choosing (consciously or unconsciously) your guiding principles. But if you're of good character, you choose those principles with humility—you don't make them up as you go along, and you respect the traditions from which you learned the principles. I don't mean that you accept traditional views without question, but that you aren't so arrogant as to think that you are wiser than traditions that have lasted generations. Indeed, the most passionate advocates of reform whom we have come to honor—think King or Gandhi—based their critiques of prevailing structures on principles derived from venerable traditions. It's the Jim Jones types (of Jonestown massacre infamy) who see themselves as the source of wisdom, with horrendous consequences.

So good character involves a commitment to principles of conduct, derived from outside of yourself, that might involve subordinating your own impulses in the moment. But I would add another requirement: good character means that your guiding principles aren't primarily based on how your behavior might be judged by others, but on right and wrong.

If you're guided mainly by how you think others will judge you, then you'll be motivated by the threat of shame, and your ethical choices will fluctuate with the prevailing breezes. But if you're guided by a sense of right and wrong—that is, morality—you'll recognize that sometimes the right thing is unpopular, and you'll strive to do it even if others disapprove. And if you choose to do the wrong but popular thing, so as to avoid public shame, you'll instead feel guilt.

The distinction between shame and guilt isn't consistent in common usage. Here I am using the term "shame" to refer to your perception of yourself as a flawed *person*, and "guilt" to refer to your perception of your *behavior* as flawed. You can feel both shame and guilt simultaneously, of course. But if you feel that you can't face anyone because you are unlovable and deserve to be shunned, you're feeling shame, not guilt. If you feel that you're fundamentally valid and loveable, but have done something you recognize as wrong and feel badly about it, you're feeling guilt, not shame.

The anthropologist Ruth Benedict, writing in the 1940s, described the concept of "shame-based" versus "guilt-based" cultures (Benedict, 1946). I think the concept has sometimes been applied too simplistically; after all, both shame and guilt affect everyone, and both have evolved as essential moderators of our social behaviors as a species. As I mentioned in Chapter 3, without shame we would have no cultural norms, and without guilt we would have no morality. Do away with either one and you have chaos.

But I think the distinction between shame-based and guilt-based systems is useful, not to divide up the world's cultures, but to examine forces that operate in each of us.

In governing your behavior, if you're primarily worried about how people will judge you—independently of right and wrong—you're mostly concerned with avoiding shame. Behavior in shame-based systems, be they families, institutions, or cultures, is dominated by concern about reputation—it's the approval of others that staves off the feeling of being unlovable. As such, in conflict, the important thing is to win. To be caught doing something outside the rules is humiliating, but if you're not caught, it's not a problem. And to be accused of something outside the rules, or to simply be affronted in some way, is an assault on your fundamental worth and calls for retaliation. There's no room for atonement; to admit wrongdoing is to accept permanent shame, and to apologize just shows weakness.[38]

Families dominated by shame tend to be abusive (at least by the standards of guilt-based systems), and people raised in such families are apt to be dominated by shame in their self-judgments. If you have a dominant position in such a family, you're prone to being a bully; and if you're in a subordinate position, you're prone to being bullied. Both bullies and bullied end up in constant fear of being shamed.[39]

---

[38] That description may seem familiar in terms of certain styles of national governance in recent years.

[39] This phenomenon extends to larger institutions as well. Greg Lukianoff and Jonathan Haidt (2018) have written about how this has played out in the "call-out" culture of many college campuses in the past few years, showing how the power of social media has been used to quickly shame people who commit small violations of ever-more exacting norms. The result has sometimes been to silence dissenting ideas.

On the other hand, if you're primarily worried about whether your actions are right or wrong, you're trying to avoid guilt. Reputation is still important in a guilt-based system—indeed, fear of shame is still a motivator. But unlike a shame-based system, in a guilt-based system it's possible to do something without anyone knowing and still feel bad (that, of course, is what guilt is). And it's possible to do something you know to be right, even when others disapprove. In a guilt-based system, you judge your actions according to internalized morals, regardless of whether you're observed or not.

The great innovation that gave rise to guilt-based systems was the assumption that our fundamental worth is a given—that we don't have to prove it. In Western religious terms based on the Hebrew Bible, this assumption follows from the idea that individuals are created *b'tzelem Elohim*, in the image of God.[40] If each of us has intrinsic worth independent of our standing with others, then our moral judgments depend less on what others think, and more on how we understand what God wants of us. As Rabbi Jonathan Sacks (2016) explains, "The emergence of a guilt culture in Judaism flowed from its understanding of the relationship between God and humankind. In Judaism we are not actors on a stage with society as the audience and the judge. We can fool society; we cannot fool God."

Moreover, in a guilt-based system, the assumption of an individual's intrinsic worth has the effect of separating the deed from the doer, which renders atonement possible. If I've done wrong and realize it, I can accept responsibility and try to repair the damage, and thereby merit forgiveness. Since we assume that we're all prone to error, you can accept your own and others' moral mistakes as part of being human, and offer forgiveness when you deem it earned. And even if other people are unable or unwilling to forgive, you can still find God's forgiveness through acts of repentance. Thus, in a guilt-based system, apology becomes emotionally possible, since apologizing isn't committing reputational suicide (as it would be in a shame-based system). It also becomes effective, as it allows you to feel whole again.

How does this translate into getting hold of yourself? As I noted earlier, to act as the person you want to be—to embody good character—is to recognize that you sometimes need to subordinate

---

[40]Genesis 1:27

your feelings and be guided by principles outside of yourself. To get hold of yourself in ways that respect your partner's dignity and integrity (as well as your own), you need to be guided more by guilt than by shame. That is, you need to have a clear sense of your own fundamental validity as a person, as well as your partner's, and then act according to what's right and wrong, rather than according to how others might view you.

This is particularly evident in situations of unequal power in a relationship. Abusive relationships are almost always enforced by shame, and, in turn, shame-based systems are prone to abuse of power. For example, if a husband lives in fear that he will be seen as weak for allowing his wife to challenge his authority, he is likely to do whatever is necessary to invalidate her and protect his own fragile sense of validity. On the other hand, if he has a clear sense of his own validity—and is therefore guided by guilt, rather than shame—he's far less likely to abuse his power, and if he does, there's at least the possibility that he'll own up to it instead of shaming or attacking his wife.[41]

When you're guided by guilt rather than shame, getting hold of yourself means that you recognize both your own and others' basic validity. If you're in a position of relatively greater power in a relationship, you use your power accountably, which means that you respond to challenges with respect even when you disagree. If you're in a position of relatively less power, you're more likely to assert yourself with confidence. In either case, getting hold of yourself allows you to tolerate the anxiety that arises when you face an important disagreement.

Getting to the Right Argument

Peter and Stella came to see me about two years into their relationship, having lived together for eight months. They were both in their mid-fifties, and had each been divorced after decades-long marriages

---

[41]Guilt-based systems don't guarantee that people in power will always behave responsibly, but they at least offer the possibility that the people they do abuse can get some measure of acknowledgment. For an example of an effective apology in the context of the #MeToo movement—a rare phenomenon—see Rao (2018). Many of the apologies that have been offered by men exposed in the #MeToo movement have been pseudo-apologies, designed more to reduce shame than to acknowledge guilt (Kuusilehto, 2018).

years before they met each other. Stella had four adult children and Peter had one, all five living out of state. Like most couples in their first session, they said they wanted to learn to communicate better. They loved each other and wanted the relationship to last, but they were looking for strategies to avoid nasty arguments.

When I asked them my usual "Why are you here now, as opposed to six months ago or six months from now?" question, Stella sighed. "We probably should have come before we moved in together. I wanted to, but Peter said we could figure this out ourselves. But the fight we had two weeks ago was really what did it for me. I told Peter we either have to get some counseling or separate, and this time he agreed to come."

Peter said he had been soured on couples therapy from his experience with his then-wife. "It just seemed to make everything worse. All we did was complain about each other, and all the counselor did was sit there and nod and tell us to express ourselves. I told Stella I'd do this, but not if it's more of the same."

Their fight two weeks before wasn't physical (they never got to that point), but it reached a level of nastiness that neither of them had experienced before, even at the worst moments of their marriages. What started as a disagreement about a dish in the sink escalated to calling each other (in various combinations) idiots, lunatics, selfish assholes, and babies. They both recognized that whatever they were fighting about, it wasn't dishes.

So what were they fighting about? Each had a host of complaints about the other, but when they expressed them—unfolded laundry, wet towels, money spent on unnecessary purchases, money refused for necessary purchases, and finally the fateful unwashed dish—they realized that they sounded trivial. They each sensed tension building between them for quite a while, though they weren't sure for how long. It had definitely been getting worse since they moved in together. What they did know was that nearly anything could set them off. The assumption of good will was seriously eroded for both of them, as each new offense supported their views of each other as uncaring, or even actively hostile.

They had met through mutual friends and fell madly in love after just a few dates. Their early sex life was "phenomenal," not least because neither of them had been sexually active for years when they met. And they both agreed that they still had good sex when they were on good enough terms to want it. The problem was that they were spending more and more time not speaking to each other.

As we talked about stability and intimacy, both Stella and Peter nodded with recognition. They both wanted the relationship to work and tried to steer clear of differences that worried them—they didn't want to threaten the stability of the relationship by raising anxiety. But that led them to avoid talking about differences between them that, as they began to realize, were at the heart of their conflicts. The fights they kept having were effective ways to shut down intimacy between them, rather than risk the anxiety of facing those differences.

Those scary differences, it turned out, were about what they wanted for their future. Stella wanted to get married, to merge their finances, and to work toward retiring together somewhere near the kids and grandkids. And she thought Peter wanted those same things—after all, he had agreed to move in with her and rent out his house, and when they talked about marriage he seemed open to the idea, with the proviso that he wanted to be settled in for a while.

But as the months passed, Peter didn't show any signs of wanting to get married—if anything, it seemed to Stella that he was becoming more distant. When she called his attention to this on several occasions, usually during an argument, he assured her that he wanted to get married and would propose to her "soon," offering some kind of condition that wasn't yet fulfilled: he was saving up for a ring, or he was waiting for the right occasion to surprise her. More recently, he had said that he still wanted to get married, but needed to see that they could stop fighting for a while.

Stella realized that her pressuring Peter just made him hesitate more. And they were both trapped by the realization that if he succumbed to her pressure, his sincerity would be called into question: was he just agreeing to shut her up, or did he really want to get married? For Peter, this meant that any time Stella asked about it, he couldn't propose marriage until enough time passed that it could be considered his own idea. For Stella, this meant that she had to suppress her urge to say something about it, even though it was on her mind pretty much every time they were together. They were stuck in mutual frustration.

Their fighting about anything and everything else protected them from facing the impasse.

As we clarified the situation in therapy, Stella and Peter were able to keep themselves calm enough to understand the impasse. That didn't solve the problem, of course, but at least it got them to the right argument. When they came back for the next session, they hadn't solved the impasse, but they said they hadn't been squabbling about things nearly as much. And their assumption of good will was beginning to return, as they were each able to appreciate the frustration of the other without attributing it to hostile motives. Their relationship was on the line, but they were tolerating the anxiety enough to stay connected while they searched for a solution.

How do you know when you've arrived at the right argument? Well, it's not always as clear at is was for Peter and Stella. You might not be able to reduce your differences to a single overriding problem. But whatever the specifics, you can tell when you're getting to the right argument because, as Peter and Stella experienced, you'll stop squabbling with each other.

This will happen for two main reasons. First, in order to get there, you have to get hold of yourself sufficiently—that is, you must be able to tolerate the anxiety that comes with facing an important, relationship-on-the-line difference without panicking. That in itself mitigates a lot of the nastiness that comes when you're in fight-or-flight mode. Second, when you get hold of yourself, your ability to understand your partner's predicament, as well as your own, rises. Empathy and squabbling are mutually exclusive.

When you do get to the right argument, it's still not easy—it's scary. You've stopped being mean to each other, but that doesn't solve the problem. Now you actually have to face it.

Sometimes, you might find that the problem isn't nearly as bad as you feared, because once you get past the anxiety, you discover that you're more willing to accommodate your partner (or vice versa) than you had realized. When you're not paralyzed by fear, the possibilities open up because you can let yourself consider options that had seemed unthinkable before. That doesn't mean you'll necessarily accede to your partner's preferences—in fact, it might become more clear that you're *not* willing to do so. But you could also find that you're able to act generously, without resentment. Getting hold of yourself allows you to act with integrity and respect, even when you're facing uncertainty.

The key to getting to the right argument is the same as the key to intimacy: you must tolerate the anxiety of difference when there's a lot at stake. Getting to the right argument is itself a form of intimacy, because you have to be honest with yourself and your partner without being distracted by panic.

And taking that risk is an act of faith.

Reflections: Getting Hold of Yourself

1. Think back to your experiences as a child in your family of origin. How often did you observe parents and siblings calming themselves and resolving conflicts? Were there others who served as role models for getting hold of themselves? How have you developed the skill yourself? Are there times when you wish you were better at getting hold of yourself?

2. Think of a time when you had a difficult interaction with someone important to you (a partner, family member, or close friend). Can you recall moments in which you were able to get hold of yourself? How did you manage to keep control?

3. How do you experience shame and guilt in your life? Can you recall a time when you felt guilty about something without feeling shame, or at least not much shame?

4. Have you ever found yourself in a nasty argument with someone, then realized later you were arguing about trivialities? Were you able to get to the right argument eventually?

PART III

AND HAVE FAITH

CHAPTER 7

WHAT IS FAITH?

Why Faith?

In Part I we discussed the importance of kindness in a relationship, not merely as the quality of treating your partner with consideration, but in the stronger sense of kinship. We talked about the two golden gifts of stability and intimacy, and how both are essential for that feeling of kinship to survive and thrive. Stability skills are about lowering (or avoiding) anxiety, and intimacy skills are about tolerating anxiety. Panic is the antithesis of both skills. To be kind, you need to not panic.

That led us to Part II, in which we explored panic and its effects, both positive and negative. We saw how efforts to avoid panic can lead to a death spiral for passion in a relationship. We then discussed the role of unhealed trauma in leaving us prone to panic, and we considered how we can heal. Since the capacity for anxiety is necessary for survival and inherent in important relationships, getting hold of yourself—that is, being able to tolerate anxiety without dissolving into panic—is a key skill for relationships. And we talked about character, guided by a moral compass based on the capacity for guilt, as a key to getting hold of yourself.

But how do you acquire the ability to get hold of yourself? To be kind, you need to not panic—but how do you not panic?

The antidote to panic is faith.

Why is a psychologist talking about faith? After all, I work with people in a secular context. I'm not a faith-based practitioner as the term is often used, and I don't assume that people who consult me adhere to any particular religion or philosophy.

But, as we'll discuss in this part of the book, I've realized over my years of practice that faith is what heals people and relationships. In particular, faith is what allows you to get hold of yourself. My definition of faith is informed by that perspective.

What is faith? Let's start with what faith is *not*, as I am using the term. Faith is not the same as religion, or a belief in God or any particular entity. I have known people of faith who don't affiliate with any religion, and religious people who (as I use the term) don't seem to be people of faith. Faith is not something you believe or think; it's not a set of facts or a particular narrative.

It's also not blind confidence in any particular prediction. It's not the feeling that "everything happens for a reason," or that everything will turn out fine. I'm also not referring to a "leap of faith," which implies a willingness to believe assertions without proof, or even in the face of contrary evidence. The faith I'm talking about doesn't require you to suspend your intelligence.

Okay, that's what faith is not. So what *is* faith?

Defining Faith

Faith is when you accept that reality is right.

When you accept reality is right? What does that mean? Let's parse that definition, starting at the end. What does it mean for reality to be "right?"

Well, I don't mean "right" as in "always desirable" or even "fair." A lot of reality is, obviously, painful and unjust (more on that below). Rather, I mean reality is "right" in two senses.

First, reality is neither crazy nor arbitrary; the state of things at this moment is a natural consequence of the state of things that led up to this very moment. Reality is right in the sense that it follows orderly laws, which you can try to infer, even though you don't have enough information to predict or explain the details much of the time. This is similar to Einstein's (1941) view of the faith of the scientist: "[S]cience can only be created by those who are thoroughly imbued with the aspiration toward truth and understanding. This source of feeling, however, springs from the sphere of religion. To this there also belongs the faith in the possibility that the regulations valid for the world of existence are rational, that is, comprehensible to reason. I cannot conceive of a genuine scientist without that profound faith."[42]

To put it another way, if the laws of physics arbitrarily changed—if, for example, when you drop your toast, it not only fails to fall butter-side down, but in fact goes up to the ceiling—you would have the sense that reality *isn't* right. Our assertion that reality is right implies that this doesn't happen—or if it does, you can try to find a rational explanation for it and adjust your understanding accordingly.

Second, reality is not merely subject to orderly laws; it's *good* that it's that way. Reality is right in the sense that it's good to be what it is.[43] Not only is reality orderly and comprehensible, but it's fundamentally good.

This idea—that reality is right in the sense of good—is a statement of value, not an assertion of fact. No amount of data can confirm or deny a judgment that reality is basically a good thing. It's not provable or disprovable. Your view of reality as good can have profound effects on how you experience the world, but it's not demonstrably true or false.

Wait a minute. How could I say that reality is good when there's obviously so much wrong in the world? How can reality be good in a world so filled with evil and suffering? What kind of fundamental goodness allows so much evil? That question has been vexing people of faith since anyone was self-aware enough to ask it. There's no fully accepted proof—logical or philosophical—that reality is good, though a lot of philosophers have twisted themselves into knots trying to prove or disprove it.[44]

But the idea that reality is fundamentally good is not an assertion to be proven; rather, it's an axiom of faith—you start from there. Faith, in our definition, says that if there's evil—as there obviously is—it must be the

---

[42]Curiously, this is also the faith implied by Genesis 1 (though this point of view would probably have surprised Einstein!). Of course, the Bible is not a science book—if you think it is, see below on fundamentalism. But, as Rabbi Jonathan Sacks (2012) notes, "the first chapter of Genesis…is the necessary prelude to science, because it represents the first time people saw the universe as the product of a single creative will, and therefore as intelligible rather than capricious and mysterious." In other words, the worldview implicit in Genesis 1 says that reality is the comprehensible result of a consistent system. You can work to understand it and apply that understanding to how you participate in it.

[43]Or, to quote the assertion in Genesis 1, repeated after each major unit of creation, "God saw that it was good." Note that the rest of the biblical narrative doesn't automatically imply that assertion; it's clearly stated, repeatedly, to convey something independently important.

[44]This is not a philosophical treatise, and (as any philosopher will readily confirm) I am not a philosopher. Look up "theodicy" if you're interested in how philosophers handle this problem.

result of forces that originate in the good. We experience death because life wouldn't be life without it. We have wickedness because we would have no freedom without it. As we'll discuss later, that doesn't mean we resign ourselves to things as they are; but it means we accept that the big picture is good, even when the results look bad from our limited perspective.

Thus, reality is right in those two senses: it's orderly and comprehensible (rather than arbitrary), and it's also fundamentally good. This incorporates the scientist's faith that you can seek truth, and the religious person's faith that truth is good.

Note that it's not what you think reality *is* that determines whether you have faith. What you believe reality *is* should be open to questioning and revision based on new information. What you believe reality *is*—what you think the facts are—is a matter of science, or at least it should be. If you refuse to take in new information because it challenges your beliefs, you're not showing faith; you're just being close-minded or superstitious. Closing your mind to new information isn't faith; it's willful blindness.

No, faith isn't about what reality *is*. Faith is about what reality *means*. Faith says reality is ours to try to understand, because it's not the result of the gods playing with us for sport. And when you (inevitably) encounter aspects of reality that you don't understand, faith says that even those aspects—even suffering and evil—are rooted in a basically good universe, and you can do your best to make things better.

Now let's consider the first part of my definition of faith—the acceptance part. If I'm saying that faith itself isn't a particular belief, what does it mean to accept that reality is right? Isn't that just believing in a good universe (or, if you're oriented toward Western religions, a good God)? What's the difference between believing and accepting?

I recognize that the terms are often used synonymously, but the kind of acceptance I'm referring to isn't based on belief in a proposition. Rather, when you accept that reality is right, you're adopting that view as axiomatic, as a basis for how you experience and understand everything else. In other words, faith isn't what you believe; faith shapes *how* you believe, experience, and act. You're still using your critical faculties to interpret what you experience. But when you do so informed by faith, your experience of the facts on the ground is different from your experience of those same facts without faith. And that difference is key to how you handle your life and your relationships.

Faith versus Fundamentalism

How does this understanding of faith relate to the faith of the devoutly religious? There had better be considerable overlap, because otherwise I should just invent a different term for what I'm talking about. Both religious and nonreligious people speak of faith as central to their understanding of religious life; to create a definition of faith that excluded that understanding would be of Humpty Dumpty-class arrogance.[45] I define faith in non-religious terms not to exclude religious faith, but to assert that faith can be expressed in other ways besides traditional religious language.

In terms of Western monotheistic religions, I think that the acceptance of God as inherently good is essentially the same idea as the faith I've defined. I'm not concerned for our purposes with theological or philosophical distinctions—I'm just saying that faith as I'm using the term isn't restricted to traditional religious concepts of faith, though it can easily include them.

Moreover, I think—as a practical matter—people of faith tend to find their way to religious communities sooner or later, because they recognize that religious traditions, for all their problems, nevertheless embody a lot of wisdom. As a religiously affiliated and active person myself, I certainly don't mean for my definition to be in any way anti-religious.

But—and this is a big but—I do intend to exclude one type of religious understanding from my definition of faith: fundamentalism, by which I mean dogmatic certainty, the conviction that there is a single set of beliefs and interpretations of reality that define truth for everyone for all time, and that any nonconforming beliefs are false and must be opposed.[46]

As I am using the terms, faith and fundamentalism are actually opposites. If you think you or any one person or set of beliefs have a monopoly on truth, you're not accepting reality; you're deluding

---

[45] *"When I use a word,' Humpty Dumpty said, in rather a scornful tone, 'it means just what I choose it to mean—neither more nor less.' 'The question is,' said Alice, 'whether you can make words mean so many different things.' 'The question is,' said Humpty Dumpty, 'which is to be master—that's all.'"* (Carroll, 1900)

[46] I realize the term "fundamentalism" has different nuances in different contexts. I'm not referring to particular sects or denominations *per se*, but rather to the rigid adherence to dogma itself. I do want to emphasize that belonging to a particular religious community doesn't automatically mean that someone is a fundamentalist in the way I'm describing. Of course, some groups are much more oriented toward fundamentalism than others.

yourself. Part of faith is accepting reality as it is, which means recognizing its vast complexity, as well as your own limitations of knowledge and understanding.

Based on this understanding, if your world view is shaped by faith, you're necessarily biased toward curiosity and respect for divergent views. That does *not* mean that faith predisposes people to an anything-goes moral relativism, or a refusal to make judgments of right and wrong just because there's no absolute standard (more on that below). But it does mean that faith is incompatible with contempt or condescension toward other viewpoints. If other traditions have evolved along with my own, there must be good reasons for it.

The recognition that reality can't be captured by any one narrative encourages humility and respect for uncertainty. The existence of other points of view isn't problematic; rather, it's a natural consequence of the human condition. We have evolved as a species to have multiple understandings of reality, and no single understanding can possibly encompass all truth. Not only do different people and different cultures display diversity, but each of us is a bundle of often conflicting attitudes. If you embrace the rightness of that reality, you're necessarily humble in claims of truth.

In contrast, fundamentalism claims certainty, which implies that deviations from whatever doctrine the fundamentalist espouses are simply wrong. Contempt ("we hate you") or condescension ("we love you so much we're going to save you from the consequences of your stupidity or ignorance") are natural results of fundamentalist programs. You can tell when people are afflicted with that kind of fundamentalism, because they have no sense of humor about it. That applies every bit as much to atheists railing against religion in general as it does to religious fanatics railing against people who have the "wrong" beliefs.[47]

As with faith, I'm not defining fundamentalism in terms of *what* you believe, but *how* you believe. Both faith and fundamentalism serve as filters for how you interpret your experience. To accept the rightness of reality—to act with faith—is to accept that our own, and anyone else's, knowledge and understanding are inevitably incomplete. To espouse fundamentalism is to reject that proposition

---

[47]The movement known as New Atheism qualifies, in my view, as fundamentalism, based on the dogmatic stance of many of its advocates. For interesting takes on this, see De Waal (2013) and Haidt (2007).

and accord infallibility to a belief system. From that perspective, faith and fundamentalism are opposites.[48]

Faith versus Resignation

If you accept that reality is right, does that mean you give up on trying to change things for the better? Not at all. That kind of dreary resignation isn't faith.

Rather, accepting reality means that you accept your part in it. There's no not-participating. Whatever you do, you're a part of the picture, be it working enthusiastically for what you consider a good cause, or giving up in despair. And accepting the rightness of that reality means that not only are you part of it, but that you're *right* to be part of it. You belong here, and what you do (or don't do) matters—it *means* something. Faith means that your existence, and everyone else's, is meaningful.

So faith is not only the opposite of the closed-mindedness of fundamentalism; it's the opposite of resignation. Faith accepts that you don't have perfect knowledge of what's right, but faith nevertheless demands your involvement in doing the best you can.[49]

Faith is a check on arrogance, in that people of faith recognize that they don't have a God's-eye view of the universe. Knowing that your own judgment is fallible means that you act with humility and accountability.

But faith is also a call to responsibility, because in a life imbued with meaning, you recognize that what you do matters. There's no ducking it: you are constantly making judgments of right and wrong, and faith calls you to act accordingly. Knowing that your actions matter means you act with commitment and resolve, as well as humility and accountability. Moral relativism—which considers moral judgments to be irrelevant because there's no objective standard to apply unerringly—is inconsistent with faith.

Absolute certainty may not be available to us, but that doesn't mean there is no truth. Accepting the rightness of reality means that you strive for truth and what's right, and you oppose falsehood and

---

[48]My own read on fundamentalism, as I view it from a Jewish perspective, is that it's essentially idolatry, because it claims divine perfection for human constructions.

[49]This idea is reminiscent of Rabbi Tarfon's aphorism from *Pirke Avot (Sayings of the Fathers)* 2:16 from the Talmud: "It is not yours to complete the work, but neither are you free to desist from it."

what's wrong when you see it. Faith is the opposite of fundamentalism's arrogance and resignation's despair.

We've defined what faith is. Now let's consider how faith helps in relationships.

Faith in Practice

Remember Doris and Ken from Chapter 2? Decades into a comfortable relationship with Ken, Doris began texting an old boyfriend, and their texts entered into territory that both Doris and Ken considered inconsistent with their marriage vows. When Ken found the texts, their marriage was thrown into crisis. Doris and Ken were our poster couple for intimacy problems in a hitherto stable marriage.

Around the same time that I began to see Doris and Ken, I met John and Millie, who proceeded to tell me a strikingly similar story. (If John had been doing the texting instead of Millie, I might have suspected that John was Doris's old boyfriend; fortunately, I didn't have to worry about that potential ethical mess, since it was Millie doing the texting.[50])

Let's look at the respective reactions of the two couples, since the contrast will illustrate how faith makes a difference in practice.

Each husband was shocked, hurt, angry, and afraid. Each wanted to save his marriage, and neither one knew how to trust his wife again. Each wife was struggling to understand what she had done, and each also wanted to save her marriage. In those respects, the couples' experiences were similar. But in my first few weeks of working with both couples, some big differences emerged.

Once he got past the initial shock, John's focus was on getting near-constant reassurance that Millie wasn't doing anything that might hurt him like that again. Millie agreed that he could check her phone at any time and made a point of showing him any texting she did. John would interrogate her repeatedly about the texts he had discovered to and from her old boyfriend, parsing each detail for a potential hidden meaning. This might go on for hours.

---

[50]If I weren't an old statistician (my career before beginning clinical training), I might invest such synchronicity with mystical significance. But my statistician's brain assures me that when you see thousands of people over the years, this sort of thing is bound to happen occasionally. And this particular situation isn't all that rare.

Millie accepted the interrogations as the price of regaining John's trust. She realized that subjecting herself to interrogation wasn't a viable long-term strategy, but she hoped that as time passed, John would feel reassured. John shared that hope, but couldn't seem to stop himself from grilling her whenever a new question occurred to him.

Both John and Millie said they just wanted to go back to how things were before the texting. From that perspective, the idea that the texting might represent something meaningful and important seemed off limits. To John, for the texting to be anything but an inexplicable aberration, a kind of temporary insanity on Millie's part, would mean that Millie didn't really love him. To Millie, it would mean having to seriously reexamine how she felt about her marriage. Both of those prospects seemed terrifying. In the meantime, the more John sought reassurance or explanations from Millie, the more Millie pulled away from him, which just reinforced his suspicions.

Ken also sought reassurance from Doris, and Doris also tried to provide it. But when they consulted me, their approach was different from the start. They both realized that going back to the way things were was neither possible nor desirable. Doris wanted to help Ken feel better—she had never intended to hurt him—but she recognized that her actions reflected something important. And Ken, as hurt as he was, also recognized that he would need to get to know Doris as she is, rather than as he wanted her to be, if there was to be any hope for their marriage. They both wanted the marriage to survive, but they realized this could happen only through growth, not denial.

Ken and Doris were showing faith, while John and Millie weren't. Both couples were dealing with scary circumstances, and both showed fear. But Doris and Ken assumed from the start that whatever either of them did, be it morally correct or not, must be meaningful on some level—there was something important about what happened. The only way either of them could have avoided that conclusion was to consider Doris either fundamentally immoral or completely insane—and they both knew she was neither. And if she was neither immoral nor crazy, then what she did must be worth understanding.

That's the essence of faith: Doris and Ken started with the assumption that their reality was fundamentally right, however painful. They were willing to confront head on the realities that John and Millie were resisting. That didn't make the work for Ken and Doris easy, but they realized early on that they would each benefit from the struggle, one way or another.

I've often heard couples express gratitude for the growth they experience after that sort of struggle. That's another indicator of faith: realizing that the pain is helping you grow. Reality is meaningful, especially when it's difficult. It's faith that allows us to tolerate anxiety in order to experience intimacy.

Reflections: What is Faith?

1. Would you call yourself a person of faith? Whether you answered yes or no, what do you mean by faith? How does your understanding fit, or not fit, the definition we described in this chapter—i.e., that faith is when you accept reality is right?

2. How has your religious upbringing (or lack thereof) shaped your experience of faith as we are defining it? Has it strengthened your acceptance that reality is right, weakened it, or done a bit of both?

3. Think of a time of crisis in your life. (If you're so fortunate that you haven't had any, be grateful!) What role did faith play in helping you through it?

CHAPTER 8

HOW DOES FAITH HELP?

Three Kinds of Faith

In Chapter 7, we considered what faith is and what it is not. By defining faith as the acceptance that reality is right, I mean to emphasize that faith isn't about any particular narrative, and it doesn't require certainty. Indeed, faith recognizes that no one narrative can completely capture the complexities of existence.[51]

So, as we discussed earlier, faith isn't about *what* you believe. What you believe is a product of your understanding and experience, and you should be open to changing what you believe based on new information. Rather, faith is about *how* you believe: specifically, faith is when you experience your life knowing that whatever reality is, there's a fundamental rightness to it.

Let's take a closer look at how faith works, especially at how it helps us tolerate the anxiety of intimacy in an important relationship.

Specifically, we'll look at three kinds of faith, all of which are important components: faith in your own validity, faith in your ability to handle what happens, and faith in the big picture.

First, you need faith in your own validity as a person. When you can self-validate, you don't need to constantly seek validation from your partner, which is not only fundamentally impossible, but also profoundly unattractive.

Faith says that your validity as a person is an axiom, not a provable or disprovable idea. You don't need evidence of it; you start from it. This faith gives you the courage to face your own desires and attend

---

[51]This is one of the defining understandings of narrative therapy (White & Epston, 1990).

to your own integrity. It means you'll let yourself know what you do and don't want. You can't possibly show up in an intimate relationship unless you're clear with yourself that you have a right to be who you are. Faith in your validity doesn't make you arrogant or rigid—in fact, you can only be flexible, considerate, and generous if you have a clear sense of your own basic validity. You can only say yes if you know you're able to say no.

Remember our two couples from the previous chapter, with similar stories of texting infidelity? Doris and Ken recognized that Doris's betrayal, painful as it was, must reflect something meaningful about her, and about their marriage. In other words, they manifested faith in their fundamental validity, not because they could prove it, but because they already assumed it.

Millie and John, by contrast, were hoping to write off Millie's actions as an aberration and go back to how things were. The prospect of examining how they each felt about themselves and their marriage was too scary, especially for John, who kept demanding that Millie somehow make his anxiety go away. They lacked faith in their own and each other's basic validity, which would have allowed—actually, not merely allowed, but *required*—them to look at the hard reality of their situation.

The second kind of faith you need is faith in your ability to handle whatever happens—also known as resilience. This faith means that even when things get difficult, you know you'll figure it out somehow, even if it hurts, and even if you have to reevaluate cherished beliefs and narratives. You might have to cope with not getting everything you want. You might even have to face the decision to break up, rather than accept the consequences of staying.

Whatever you decide, you'll need to accept responsibility for your own decisions, and that requires faith in your resilience. Whatever limitations are imposed on you by circumstance—and there are always limitations—it's up to you to make the best of it. This faith gives you the courage to make hard decisions while acting with strength and clarity.

Faith in their resilience was what allowed Ken and Doris to work in therapy without any certainty about the outcome; they just knew that they'd figure it out. A lack of that faith kept John and Millie stuck where they were because the prospect of change was too terrifying to contemplate.

The third kind of faith you need is faith in the big picture, in the fundamental rightness of reality as a whole, however painful or incomprehensible it can be at times. In short, you need faith that your life has purpose. This means you can see your life, your love, and your identity as meaningful parts of something much bigger than you and your partner.[52] This faith gives you the courage to live by your values and act with commitment and dedication; it means you experience your life as meaningful, even when it's hard. This faith often manifests itself as gratitude for the growth you experience after overcoming an obstacle.

The three kinds of faith allow you to act with confidence, resilience, and purpose. You can stand up for what's important to you while still being kind, respectful, and generous to your partner. Instead of shutting yourself down, you can take a risk and discuss your desires with your partner, even if you're not sure how they will react. You can cope with the inevitable difficulties with strength and resolve. And through it all, you can experience your life as meaningful—you'll know that you're a part of something much bigger than yourself and your partner.

How Do You Develop Faith?

You need faith. But what if you don't have it? How do you get it if you haven't got it?

Faith isn't a commodity. As we've discussed before, faith isn't a set of beliefs that you can be convinced of, and it's not a set of facts that you can acquire by study or prove by scientific research. Faith isn't *what* you believe, but *how* you believe. It's not knowledge, it's a skill. And like any skill, you develop faith by practicing it.

That means making a choice to develop that skill. You start by choosing faith, rather than despair or cynicism, and then you practice making that choice over and over.

Choosing faith means recognizing that the choice is available to you. Even that step—recognizing that the choice is available—is itself an expression of faith. The idea that you can choose faith—that you can decide to accept that reality is right as an act of will—is the beginning of faith.

---

[52]We'll develop this idea further in Chapter 10.

As with other skills, it helps to find teachers, get close to people of faith, and see faith in action. Where can you find teachers? You might discover teachers of faith in religious settings, though you should take care to distinguish faith from fundamentalism, as we discussed in Chapter 7. Your own tradition is often a good place to start, since you already speak its language.

Some therapists and other health care practitioners can also teach faith, whether or not they use the word. Just as in religious settings, you need to beware of fundamentalism in health care contexts, where it can mean reducing experiences to symptoms, and an inability to see suffering as meaningful. But I've met many practitioners who embody the idea of faith in their work.

You probably already know people, in all sorts of settings, from whom you can study faith and how it manifests in practice. You can tell because when you're with them, you sense acceptance, respect, humility, reverence, wonder, appreciation, and gratitude. These are attitudes of faith. The more you experience them—the more you open your heart and mind to them—the more you acquire those attitudes yourself.

What does it mean to choose faith in real life, in the context of a relationship? What are the practical effects?

It means that you accept your own validity, so you don't need to prove it. You get less reactive with your partner, since you're not constantly seeking their validation. You stop throwing tantrums or giving your partner the silent treatment. Maybe you realize that you're triggered by old traumas, and you seek therapy to work on healing them. Maybe you realize that you've been using substances or other addictions as a way of avoiding the anxiety of real life, and you seek treatment if you need to.[53]

And if your partner is throwing tantrums, you're less susceptible to them. You stop being intimidated, and you recognize that you can leave the relationship if you need to for the sake of your own safety and dignity. But oddly enough, when you stop being intimidated, you can also be more understanding and patient with your partner. Basically, you grow up.

---

[53]Twelve-step programs such as Alcoholics Anonymous incorporate faith as a central part of their program. Though my definition of faith and the twelve-step idea of a higher power are stated differently, I think there's a lot of overlap.

Getting hold of yourself in that way challenges your partner to do the same. Whether or not your partner can rise to the occasion is up to them, but *you're* participating differently. Your old patterns stop trapping you. You come alive again.

And that's when things get interesting, because when you come alive and risk honesty with yourself and your partner, your relationship will change. Exactly how it will change isn't always predictable—that's why you need resilience. But it will change. Even just one of you coming alive and getting hold of yourself after years of being stuck creates a crisis—a crisis that will either rejuvenate the relationship or help you decide to make other plans.

Maybe you'll find that you can risk letting yourself love your partner again, rather than shutting down to protect yourself from hurt. When you respect your own validity and recognize that you're not as fragile as you feared, you'll also find that you can forgive your partner's imperfections and acknowledge your own (more on that in Chapter 9). You'll stop waiting to feel completely relaxed with your partner, and you'll realize that it's up to you if you want to connect or not. You can risk rejection by offering yourself, or you can be clear that you will no longer accept being stuck in a deep-freeze. You can even decide to accept the relationship as it is, without pressing for greater intimacy. But you'll accept responsibility for your choice, whatever it is, and stop blaming your partner for what you've chosen.

As I said, you have to develop the skill of faith by choosing it, time after time, day after day. You know you're at a crossroads when you're feeling anxious, especially around your partner, and you're feeling the urge to blame, shut down, or act out. That's the moment you need to choose faith—the three kinds of faith in your validity, resilience, and purpose. That's when choosing faith will allow you to stay present, tolerate anxiety, and offer the possibility of healing in your relationship.

Reflections: How Does Faith Help?

1. How does faith in your own validity contrast with the experience of shame? If you've experienced abuse, especially as a child, what effects did the abuse have on your faith in your own validity? How can shame affect your ability to be clear with yourself and with a partner about what's important to you in a relationship?

2. Think of an occasion when someone you know showed resilience in the face of difficult circumstances. How did this affect your feelings about them? Now think about a time you showed resilience yourself. How did this affect your feelings about yourself?

3. Who has taught you faith? Consider not only teachers and parents who explicitly instructed you, but also people from whom you learned faith just by being around them and observing how they interact with the world.

CHAPTER 9

FAITH AND FORGIVENESS

What is Forgiveness, and Why Forgive?

Over the years I've worked with many people who have been badly hurt. Some seem to hold on to the bitterness and anger for years. But I've met many people who've been able to forgive: the woman who forgave her father for brutally abusing her as a child; the father who forgave his son for stealing from him, lying to him and about him, and assaulting him; the man who forgave the drunk driver for killing his daughter; and, not uncommonly, people who forgave their spouses for cheating.

What is it about these people that allows them to forgive the most horrible wrongs? Are they crazy? In denial? Weak-minded?

Let's talk about what forgiveness is, and what it is not—because it turns out that those people who are capable of forgiving aren't crazy at all. They've found a path to emotional freedom.

What is forgiveness? Like faith, the word is used in different ways and in different contexts. For our purposes, forgiveness means letting go of the bitterness, the resentment, the anger, and thoughts of revenge—it means letting go of the pain that you've been carrying since you were hurt.[54]

You'll know you've forgiven when you still feel at peace even when you're reminded of the hurt. You can think about the hurt with compassion for yourself, for people who've been similarly hurt, and even for those who hurt you. You won't excuse, justify, or minimize

---

[54]You might note the similarity between forgiveness as we're defining it here, and healing from trauma as we discussed in Chapter 5. As we'll discuss below, that's not mere coincidence. Healing from trauma is a prerequisite for forgiveness.

the wrong that was done to you; but you'll understand it with a mature perspective.

And when you've forgiven, you may even feel a sense of gratitude when you think about the hurt: gratitude that you survived, that you learned from the experience, and that your spirit is now free of it.

Let's look carefully at what forgiveness is *not*. Forgiveness doesn't mean that the person who did the wrong is absolved of responsibility for what they did, morally, legally, or interpersonally. We're not talking about "forgiving a debt," which is when a person no longer has to pay what they owe. (Indeed, you could release someone from a debt but not forgive them at all.)

Forgiving someone also doesn't mean you've decided their actions weren't so bad after all. You can forgive someone and still think that what they did was completely and seriously wrong. Of course, sometimes people do reconsider their judgments of someone's behavior and they decide that it wasn't so bad; the point at the moment is that forgiveness doesn't *have to* imply a change in your moral calculus.

Forgiving definitely does not mean forgetting; it means you've been through whatever it was, and you've learned from it. In fact, if you've really forgotten about something, there's nothing to forgive.[55]

And forgiving someone doesn't mean you're going to continue your relationship with them. Whether or not you continue a relationship depends on trust, and forgiving someone doesn't mean that you'll trust them in any way—trust is a different issue entirely. I've known people who have forgiven abusive exes, but still maintain restraining orders against them. Forgiveness doesn't make you stupid.

Similarly, forgiving someone does not require that they accept responsibility for their actions, or that they apologize. Forgiveness has nothing to do with whether the offender deserves it. You can forgive someone who is completely unrepentant, though that can be emotionally more difficult, since you're likely to feel anger at their lack of remorse. Feeling that someone is genuinely sorry is important when deciding whether you should trust them, but their repentance is not necessary for you to forgive them.

---

[55]For example, I've heard several stories of people who received abject apologies at school reunions for offenses they had no memory of. They generally say there's no need to forgive—they haven't been carrying it around.

So, why should you forgive when you've been hurt? What difference does forgiveness make if it doesn't absolve the offender morally, repair the relationship, or signify renewed trust?

The reason you should forgive is, in essence, the same reason for which you should have faith. Actually, forgiveness is an act of faith, because in forgiving someone, you acknowledge that what happened to you is part of a bigger picture, one that you accept as right. Forgiveness is a way to stop insisting that reality be different from what it is. Yes, you were hurt, but you can heal from the hurt, and benefit from what you learned along the way.

Forgiveness is about you, not whoever hurt you. When you forgive, you let go of the pain, regardless of whether you choose to continue the relationship or trust the other person.

Three Steps to Forgiveness

How do you get there? How did those people I mentioned manage to let go of the hurt, to move past the bitterness, even toward those who had done terrible things?

Well, first you need to determine if you're ready to forgive, because you might not be. If you're still being hurt in your relationship—say, you're deciding whether to separate from an abusive partner, or your partner dumped you recently and you're trying to get over the hurt— then forgiveness may be premature, because you might still need to hang on to the anger for a while. I've known couples who have mutually decided to divorce (i.e., no apparent "dumper" or "dumpee"), but they still needed to be angry with each other for a while, to help them separate emotionally.

Forgiving is also difficult when you're dealing with unhealed trauma, for similar reasons: the unhealed trauma means that you're still being hurt in the present, even though the event may have occurred far in the past. Anger toward the abuser is often an important step in healing. If you're dealing with unhealed trauma, you're probably not ready to forgive.

Moreover, you're the only one who can decide when you're ready to forgive. Family, friends, and therapists may all mean well by urging you to forgive, since they see the pain you're in. The person who hurt you might also urge you to forgive them, and it's natural for them to want this. But only you can forgive—and only you can decide when you're ready.

How do you know you're ready? You know you're ready to forgive when you realize that the pain you're hanging on to is your own—it no longer has anything to do with what anyone else did or didn't do. You're ready to forgive someone when it's no longer about them—it's about you. Forgiveness is about you. That's the key to being ready and able to forgive.

You get there in three steps: forgiving yourself, forgiving those who hurt you, and forgiving God. As we'll see, these three steps correspond to the three kinds of faith we talked about in Chapter 8. Let's consider each step.

Forgiving Yourself

First, forgive yourself. To really forgive, to let go of the hurt, you must forgive yourself—because when you're hurt, you almost always blame yourself for part of it, whether it's reasonable to do so or not.

Of course, sometimes your self-blame is justified. Sometimes, you come to realize that you also hurt the person who hurt you, that it's not all one way. And maybe you need to face that courageously, forgive yourself, and then offer an apology for what you did. (If you want to ask for forgiveness from someone you hurt, you need to understand that they might not be ready to forgive you.)

But sometimes, you might blame yourself even when you didn't do anything wrong, when the only way you could have done something different required power or knowledge that you couldn't have had at the time.

There's an emotional logic to this phenomenon. Blaming yourself implies a belief that you could have done something differently. How does this help? Consider how life would be if you felt you were constantly at the mercy of forces over which you had no control at all. From an evolutionary perspective, we've done better as a species by assuming that we have more influence than we actually do, since this causes us to panic less.[56]

---

[56]That would explain the survival value of superstitions, for example.

Moreover, many of our mental processes operate with no sense of time. (Dreams are a good example.) When you've been hurt, part of you just wants to erase the event. That part feels—no, it knows—that if you just went back and did things differently, you could avoid the hurt. Of course, the reality of time says you can't do that. Self-blame is, in part, an effort to go back and change history.

Self-blame is particularly common if you were abused as a child, because the abuser almost certainly forced it on you: you were told that it was your fault, that no one would believe you, that you're dirty, bad, or worthless. As an adult, you might recognize that you were a child, and that you were being overpowered and threatened, but still blame yourself emotionally for not simply ending it, the way you might have been able to do as an adult. Again, this isn't realistic, but to feel otherwise is to accept the idea that abuse is unavoidable. And instead of accepting that, you give yourself the illusion that you had some control over it by blaming yourself. Looking at it this way, self-blame is a protection against despair. If it's my fault, maybe I can do something about it.

Fundamentally, forgiving yourself means recognizing that you actually can't change what happened in the past—you did the best you could, given who you were and what was happening. It's easy to look back and see what you might have done differently, if you or the situation had been different. But forgiving yourself means accepting that you and the situation weren't different. It was what it was.

If you're dealing with unhealed trauma, that realization can be terrifying, because it feels as if the traumatic event is still happening. That's why it's hard to forgive yourself until you've healed from the trauma; to accept that you aren't to blame requires you to accept that the event happened, and that you couldn't stop it. If it feels like it's still happening, that's a recipe for panic or despair.

When you have healed and can accept the reality of what happened, you can have compassion for who you were back then. That's what it means to forgive yourself. And in accepting that you were powerless to stop whatever happened, you can then look realistically at the power you actually do have now. If you were a child when you were hurt, you can recognize that you now have adult power, so you can't be hurt as a child again. And even if you were hurt as an adult, you can recognize that you've learned from the experience—you know more now than you did then, and that knowledge can protect you in the future.

Forgiving yourself means having faith in your own validity (as we discussed in Chapter 8). When you stop blaming yourself for doing the best you could, given what power and knowledge you had at the time, you're accepting your own validity as a person.

Forgiving Those Who Hurt You

Which leads us to the second step: forgiving those who hurt you.

Actually, this one is theoretically simple, once you've forgiven yourself. Forgiving yourself means accepting that it was what it was, and you can get past the pain and regret for your own actions. When you can do that, it's not much harder to accept the same about whoever hurt you.

You don't have to justify what they did, approve of it, or excuse it; to forgive, you just have to accept that they were who they were at that moment, and it was what it was. You no longer have to wish it away. You can understand that people sometimes do bad things, and though you try, sometimes you can't prevent it. You realize that even perpetrators of horrible crimes are human—we all have that in common. That's what it means to forgive whoever hurt you.

As we noted earlier, this in no way implies that you'll be able to trust whoever hurt you, or that you'll maintain a relationship with them. It just means that you don't need to carry the pain anymore.

This step—forgiving those who hurt you—is nearly impossible to do until you've forgiven yourself. That's why I'm describing the process of forgiveness as involving sequential steps. If you're taking the blame for someone else's actions, you might think you've forgiven them, but that's just denying the hurt they've caused you. To forgive someone, by definition, means they did something that needs forgiving. Even if you share the guilt for what happened, trying to forgive someone else without first forgiving yourself won't help you let go of the anger; you're just dissociating from it. To forgive someone means you have to feel worthy of forgiveness.

Forgiving those who hurt you corresponds to the second kind of faith: resilience, or the faith that you can handle what happens. To let go of the pain is to accept that bad things can (and did) happen, and that you can deal with it. You no longer have to protest against reality; you have faith that you can work with it, even when it's bad.

Forgiving God

There's one more step in forgiveness. When you've been badly hurt, you ultimately need to forgive God. If the idea of "God" is problematic for you, just think of it as a shorthand way of referring to the third kind of faith: faith in the big picture, which implies a sense of meaning and purpose in your life.

Why would you need to forgive God?

You need to forgive the fact that we exist as conscious beings with some amount of influence, some tantalizing sense that we can control our lives, and yet we still get hurt—badly. You need to forgive the fact that we've developed moral and ethical values that improve our relationships and help us rise above our narrow interests, and yet we still see good people get hurt and bad people get away with it. Even if you're an atheist, I suspect you often feel that God's got some serious explaining to do for the mess in this world.

That's *why* you need to forgive God: until you do, you're essentially resenting existence itself, which renders life meaningless and miserable. But *how* do you forgive God? And wouldn't that mean accepting the unacceptable?

There's no formula for forgiving God, just as there's no formula for developing faith. Of course, I juxtapose the two because forgiving God is, as I use the terms, equivalent to developing faith. When you've forgiven God, you've accepted reality as a whole—not with dreary resignation, but with a sense that reality is right, even when it's painful, and even as you dedicate yourself to repairing it and healing the pain.

As we discussed in Chapter 8, that kind of faith isn't a commodity to acquire, but a skill to develop. You choose it, you find teachers, you learn from traditions, and you practice. It's a life-long project.

Forgiveness and Intimacy

We've been talking about why and how to forgive in general. Now let's focus on forgiveness in the context of an ongoing committed relationship: what does it take to forgive your partner when they've hurt you?

Let's revisit our couples from Chapters 7 and 8. Recall Doris and Ken, who came to see me soon after Ken discovered Doris's texts to an old boyfriend, and also John and Millie, who had a very similar story.

As we discussed in Chapter 8, both couples were in crisis. But Ken and Doris were able and willing to look at what happened with the assumption that they needed to learn and grow from the experience. As angry as Ken was initially, he knew that what Doris did must reflect something meaningful, and as surprised as Doris was about her own behavior, she also recognized that she needed to consider what it meant. They manifested faith—not certainty that their marriage would survive, but faith that whatever happened, they would learn from it.

Hearing Doris describe her experience of their marriage and how she found herself texting her old boyfriend was painful for Ken. As he listened to her, he recognized that both of them had inadvertently conspired to avoid intimate connection for years.

He was particularly distressed to hear of Doris's frustration and boredom with their sex life. She had never explicitly told Ken about those feelings, and hadn't consciously realized them herself until her texting became sexual and she felt what she was missing. Ken knew he had been the more uptight one when it came to talking about sex—he could think of times when Doris tried to say something, but he had always found ways to change the subject.

For Ken to open himself up to Doris's experience, and consider his own part in shaping their marriage, meant that he had largely forgiven her. It wasn't all at once, and it wasn't every moment, but he stopped being consumed by anger every time he thought about what she had done.

That didn't mean he condoned her actions. He still thought what she did was wrong, even in the context of a marriage starved for intimacy—and so did Doris, for that matter. And his forgiving her didn't mean that he was sure he wanted to stay with her. It just meant that he could be honest with himself and open to honesty from her.

For Doris to acknowledge how much she craved intimacy after so many years of suppressing her feelings meant that she had to forgive herself—to accept her own validity—as well as forgive Ken for his part in their mutual avoidance of intimacy. She wasn't condoning her actions; but by understanding the context, she was able to be clearer with herself and with Ken about what happened, and about why she wouldn't do it again.

As our work progressed, Ken and Doris both began to express gratitude for what they were going through because they saw how much more honest their relationship had become. Again, this didn't presuppose that they were going to stay together—but it meant that they were able to hear each other, even when it was difficult. The experience allowed for intimacy between them as they considered how to heal.

In contrast, Millie and John were nowhere near forgiving each other as our work began. For John, the thought of what Millie had done was infuriating. But rather than trying to understand what she did, John obsessed about making sure she didn't do it again. In his view, Millie owed him whatever he needed to feel reassured. He wasn't interested in hearing how she felt—whatever she said about her feelings was just an excuse for her bad behavior. He felt her apologies were insufficient and insincere; he knew he wanted to stay with her, but forgiving her seemed impossible. He just wanted to know it wouldn't happen again, so he could "forget about it and move on."

Millie was also in favor of forgetting about it and moving on. She hoped that by yielding to John's demands for ever more detailed answers and constant surveillance of her phone use, he would get what he needed and stop harassing her. She also wanted to save the marriage, and her explanation for what she had done was simply that she had made a mistake and wouldn't do it again.

By trying to forget about what had happened, neither Millie nor John were allowing for the possibility that Millie's texting represented a valid issue. They both wanted to feel better, but the fear of what might happen if they actually listened to themselves and each other was more than they could tolerate. They could not forgive because they could not face reality, and intimacy between them was going to be impossible unless they were able to risk the anxiety of doing so.

Just as it was for Ken and Doris, risking intimacy wouldn't mean that John and Millie would necessarily stay together. But it would mean that they could face the situation with integrity and courage. Our work would turn on whether we could facilitate that.

Reflections: Faith and Forgiveness

1. Is there someone in your life who hurt you, whom you have forgiven? If so, what allowed you to forgive them? Recall, if you can, how you felt along the way as you worked toward forgiveness. How did your relationship with the person change when you forgave them?

2. Have you forgiven anyone with whom you couldn't reestablish trust—say, an ex who cheated on you?

3. Are there people who have hurt you whom you have not forgiven, in the sense that you still get angry when you're reminded of them? What has prevented you from forgiving them? Is the hurt too recent? Are you experiencing unhealed trauma from the hurt? Or does your anger serve some other purpose?

Where to Now?

We've talked about each of the three parts of the seven-word formula: be kind, don't panic, and have faith.

In Part I we focused on kindness, as in the sense of kinship that keeps you coupled. We talked about the two golden gifts of stability and intimacy, and the skill sets you need to develop them: character for stability, and tolerance of anxiety for intimacy. And we noted that both of those skill sets require that you be able to manage panic.

In Part II we considered panic and its effects on relationships, tracing how efforts to avoid anxiety for the sake of stability often lead to a loss of intimacy. We talked about unhealed trauma as a particular source of panic, and ways of healing it. Since getting hold of yourself is the quintessential skill that lets you be kind, we talked about how you can develop that skill. We explored how your sense of entitlement is a major determinant of how and when you freak out (or don't), and we considered the roles of shame and guilt in shaping your reactions. And we considered what happens when you're able to get to the right argument, which requires you to tolerate the anxiety of staying with a problem you don't know how to solve—and that itself requires faith that you can find a way forward.

That led us to Part III, in which we explored the role of faith as the antidote to panic. We talked about what faith is and isn't, distinguishing faith from both fundamentalism and resignation. And we described the role of forgiveness in relationships as a manifestation of faith.

Having focused in Parts I through III on the seven-word formula—what each part means, and how the three principles fit together—we'll now put it to work. In Part IV we'll apply the principles to some of the most common issues that arise between couples, and which often bring them to therapy: marriage, sex, infidelity, and breakups.

PART III

NOW GO AND LEARN

CHAPTER 10

WHY GET MARRIED?

Why should you get married?

Nowadays, most of the traditional reasons to get married are no longer valid.

How about sex? At least for the vast majority of people living in North America and Western Europe, there is very little social stigma attached to consensual, non-marital sex. The usual advice nowadays is to be sure you're sexually compatible with someone before marrying them, so you certainly don't need to get married just to have sex.

What about having children? Well, having children outside of marriage is now close to the norm. In recent years, about 40 percent of births in the United States were born to unmarried mothers (National Center for Health Statistics, 2019). And among those births, an increasing percentage of them are born to couples who live together (ChildTrends, 2018). So there are more and more people living together as couples—people who presumably could marry each other if they wanted to—who are having children without getting married. There's little social pressure to get married just because you're pregnant. The "shotgun wedding" is becoming a relic.

Even the legal protections of marriage aren't all that difficult to replicate in other ways, at least for many purposes. In the United States, unmarried people can hold property and money in common, adopt children together, designate each other as health care proxies, and name each other as beneficiaries. You might pay more in taxes as an unmarried couple, but there are some circumstances in which you might actually pay more if you get married.

Yes, there are some legal reasons why marriage is helpful—but that's not what most couples are wondering when this topic comes up in my office. Usually, we arrive at the topic because one of them wants to get married while the other doesn't, and neither has been able to find a convincing enough argument.

So why *should* you get married, if you can live pretty much the same way unmarried?

Spoiler alert: I think marriage is important, and there are powerful reasons for entering into it—but I don't think it's for everyone. So I'm going to start with some reasons why maybe you *shouldn't* get married.

Why You Shouldn't Get Married

First, if you think getting married guarantees a lasting relationship, think again. The chance of an American marriage ending in divorce these days is actually not quite 50 percent, but somewhere in the forties. Surely you know lots of divorced people; it's not at all uncommon.

And of course, marriage doesn't guarantee fidelity (see Chapter 12). Lots of married people cheat on their spouses. Even though marriage represents a promise to stay married and faithful to each other, it often doesn't turn out that way.

And if you think that getting married will reduce conflict between you and your partner, you're sorely mistaken. The only argument that marriage can reliably eliminate is the one about whether or not you should get married. And in exchange, getting married often intensifies the other conflicts you're already having, because the stakes are higher.

I've worked with many couples who have gotten locked into a dance with each other: She wants to get married and is constantly fighting with her partner because he won't propose; and he won't propose because they're fighting so much. She thinks if they'd just get married, it would end the conflict. He thinks if she'd just not be so fixated on marriage, it would end the conflict. Usually it turns out they're both wrong—whether they get married or not, they're still going to deal with conflict.

Here are some other bad reasons to get married:

Don't get married because it's the obvious next step in your relationship, or because it means you're really committing to each other, or because you don't feel like a complete person if you're not married. Marriage might be the obvious next step, but the obvious next step sometimes turns out to be a nasty stumble. Commitment can be just as valid without marriage—indeed, it better be, because marriage doesn't guarantee anything about how you'll feel toward each other in the long haul.

And if you think marriage will make you a more complete person, you're in for a rude awakening. Once you face the reality that you actually have differences with your "other half"—maybe painful ones—you'll have to handle your anxiety on your own. If you can't get hold of yourself—*by* yourself—don't get married.

Even your love for each other—your sense of being a team, of having each other's back, of being willing to sacrifice for each other, of joy in each other's presence, of ecstatic connection—that kind of love—isn't a good enough reason to get married. You can feel that way without marriage, and marriage doesn't guarantee that it will last.

Well, that's a pretty dismal view of marriage, isn't it? But as I said, I think marriage is very important, at least for many people. So, what *should* prompt you to get married?

Why You Should Get Married

You should get married when you realize it's not about you.

Marriage isn't about you, your partner, or even the two of you as a couple. Marriage is a commitment to something outside of you, a deep acceptance of responsibility to do your part in the big picture.

Of course, you don't have to be married to be a responsible person, or to be committed to your part in the big picture. Anyone, married or single, can and should do that. I act responsibly in any context when I recognize that everything isn't about me—when I'm willing to subordinate my own comfort or interest to the needs of the whole.

What I'm saying is, the reason to get married is that you want to put your relationship in that same category. To get married is to commit your love, and your life as a couple, to a higher cause. It's not about how much you love each other, or how happy your relationship makes you feel. It's not about you. It's bigger than that. And if it isn't, don't get married.

Here's another way of saying it: marriage isn't a contract, it's a covenant. Contracts are agreements about mutual benefit. Covenants are commitments built into your sense of self, and they're about much more than mutual benefit. You enter into a covenant as an expression of your deepest values. In the case of marriage, those values involve relationships with family, community, and humanity in general that are, in large measure, not yours to define. When you get married, you're accepting that others—other people, other families and communities, even other legal systems—have a role in defining and shaping your relationship. It's not about you.

Marriage ceremonies in Jewish, Christian, and Islamic traditions incorporate this idea explicitly by emphasizing that marriage forms a relationship sanctified by God. But you don't have to be religious in the traditional Western sense to understand this concept. When you get married, you're voluntarily accepting that something much bigger than you and your partner is involved. You're taking on a new identity in the world; it's not merely coincidental that marriages are public events, often sanctified in ceremonies that explicitly recognize the role of the larger community in supporting the couple.[57]

This explains why the right to marry has historically been so important to people who were denied it in the past, such as interfaith, interracial, or same-sex couples. Marriage represents something much bigger than simply celebrating a couple's love; it's not about them. It's about everyone.

Many of the couples I've met who are struggling with the decision to get married understand this intuitively, even if they might have difficulty articulating it. It's not just a "piece of paper from the City Hall," to quote Joni Mitchell.[58] If it were, they wouldn't be struggling with it.

But I've also met many couples who are surprised by how much marriage matters, often not realizing it until after they're married. And sometimes, they realize they had no idea what they signed up for. Marriage can be wonderfully reassuring and comforting, in that it connects you to something greater; but for the same reason, marriage intensifies the anxiety you feel when important differences emerge.

---

[57]Jewish marriage ceremonies are performed under a *chupa*, a canopy open on all sides to symbolize the role of the broader community in the creation of the new couple.

[58]Joni Mitchell, *My Old Man*

Marriage, Anxiety, and Stability

Of course, one source of anxiety that comes with marriage, at least for most people, is the idea that you're committing to one person for life.[59] Yes, divorce is available as a remedy if you determine you've made a mistake, but divorce is difficult by design, both legally and emotionally. Indeed, the difficulty of divorce is itself a reflection of the importance of marriage.

That's one of the main reasons people choose to form partnerships, including as parents, without getting married: to avoid marriage is to avoid the anxiety of potential divorce. I've heard many people (usually men, though not always) express that view, often coupled with an observation that many of their friends were just fine in their relationships until they got married, at which time everything went to hell.

To use the terms we've established in this book, a decision to avoid marriage in a committed monogamous relationship makes sense from the standpoint of stability: you're avoiding a major source of anxiety. Knowing you can get out of the relationship if you want to—not easily, but much more easily than if you were married—means you don't feel trapped. This, in theory, could mean that you're better prepared to handle the ups and downs of the relationship without splitting up. Therefore, many people avoid marriage not because they aren't committed to their partners, but, paradoxically, because they *are* committed, and they don't want to compromise the stability of the relationship by raising the stakes.[60]

---

[59]Of course, this presumes that both parties want monogamy, and that they intend for the marriage to be a lifetime partnership. There are obvious exceptions—for example, couples who marry for health insurance, immigration status, or to escape abusive or oppressive situations—but I'm focusing on the vast majority of couples I see in my office, who intended a monogamous lifetime commitment when they got married. Even couples who don't presume sexual exclusivity typically, in my experience, still intend that marriage represent a partnership that is exclusive in some sense, such as emotional intimacy.

[60]Whether that logic works out in practice, statistically, is unclear. You can find lots of studies that show that, at least in the USA and UK, cohabitation is less stable than marriage, though some of those studies focus on people who cohabit before marrying. But other, more recent studies show contradictory findings (Fetters, 2018). One study (Kuperberg, 2016) showed that much of the apparent negative effect of premarital cohabitation was explainable by age: people who cohabit before marrying tended to be younger.

So the question of whether getting married is likely to increase or decrease the stability of your relationship, at least in statistical terms, has no definitive answer. Of course, the people I've met who feel that marriage would threaten their relationship—and there have been many—aren't basing those feelings on statistical studies. My point is that their feeling that way is neither unusual nor illogical.

As we've already discussed in several contexts, avoiding anxiety for the sake of stability is fine, unless you're avoiding the anxiety that comes with intimacy. Is there a cost in intimacy to avoiding marriage? Or, to put it another way, how might marriage allow for greater intimacy than living together unmarried?

Marriage and Intimacy

Marriage doesn't allow for greater intimacy if you see it as a restriction. The sense that you're trapping yourself with one person and denying yourself all sorts of enticing alternatives for the rest of your life doesn't encourage intimacy; it encourages panic.

But there's another way to experience marriage. What if joining together as a married couple forms a new organism, one that is alive and interacting with the world as an entity, with a mind that is more than the sum of its parts? Just as each person comprises many internal systems, each of which is somewhat independent but affects the others, a couple comprises two persons: both somewhat independent, but affecting each other. And just as the systems within a person develop and grow to form a living entity with its own mind, so do the two persons in a couple: the couple itself becomes a living entity that acts, in some ways, with a mind of its own.

You can understand any sort of complex system in that way, of course, at whatever level you wish: families, villages, cultures, nations, even entire species can each be considered living organisms.[61] But from an individual's perspective, a married couple is the one higher-level organism that you can most readily choose or decline to become a part of, at least if you live in a culture that permits you that choice.[62] You can't choose the family into which you were born, or the culture in which you were raised; but, if you're fortunate, you can choose to get married or not.

---

[61] Even the universe as a whole can be considered a mind. See, for example, Goff (2018).

[62] Of course, in many cultures, men have far more choice than women about whether to get married. Even in the culture in which I work, in the USA, men are far more apt to express doubts about marriage than women. Only recently in human history could women perceive marriage as an individual option, particularly given the economic vulnerability that unmarried women have traditionally faced.

To choose to be part of a larger system is, in part, to give up some individual autonomy. That's certainly true of marriage. But as part of that larger system, you experience levels of intimacy—of connection with the wider world—both as an individual and as part of the larger system. You grow and change as an individual, but you also grow and change along with the larger system. It's in this sense that marriage offers a level of intimacy not available if you remain single.[63]

How does marriage-level intimacy affect you in practical terms? What do you get from being part of something bigger than yourself? Well, consider what changes once you get married. Whether you're aware of it or not, your family, friends, coworkers, and larger communities immediately experience you not only as yourself, but as part of the couple unit. So how you're doing as a couple suddenly becomes everybody's business, whether you like it or not. "How are you?" takes on a different meaning, both singular and plural. Your interface with the world has expanded: now it's not just about what you experience as an individual, but also what both of you experience, together or not. In this way, you're more richly connected to the world.

In particular, you'll acquire a new set of family relationships, with all their embedded expectations and assumptions, which might be very different from the ones you grew up with in your own family. Since a lot of those expectations and assumptions relate to what people in the family do—i.e., married, not just living together—you'll bump into differences between you and your partner that don't tend to manifest until you get married.

In other words, marriage makes you kin, not just voluntary associates. The intimacy that marriage offers is the intimacy of kinship, which is at a different level than the intimacy of individuals. You're involved in the world both as individuals and as a kinship unit—and you don't get to define how that plays out.

Sound scary? Indeed, the anxiety that accompanies marriage-level intimacy is precisely what people are trying to avoid by declining marriage. But, as we discussed in Chapter 1, we couple for kindness because we crave kinship. You don't have to get married to

---

[63]Similarly, people who enter monastic orders take on restrictions so as to participate in the higher-level intimacy of the order as a whole. Catholic nuns are inducted into their orders with a marriage ceremony.

find a sense of kinship: devoting yourself as a committed member of any group can give you some of it. But marriage represents the quintessential way we have evolved to bring that sense of kinship to an otherwise optional relationship.

For many people, the issue of marriage is never a question because they are so naturally oriented to marriage—to finding not just mutual love and companionship, but also kinship—that you might as well ask why their hair should grow. It's just what humans do, and they don't see any reason to be conflicted about it. But, as I implied earlier, if you're particularly interested in this chapter, it's probably because you're not sure, or someone you care about isn't sure.

So, why get married? Don't get married because you think it will make you more secure, because it probably won't. If you marry, you'll be subject to a whole new set of potential anxieties.

But if you can handle those anxieties, marriage offers a path to a kind of transcendent intimacy, a sense of higher purpose and meaning in your life. Marriage is not about you, but about dedicating yourself and your relationship to that higher purpose. If that's the path you want to choose, then get married.

Reflections: Why Get Married?

1. If you've been married, why did you get married, instead of just living together? Did you talk about that question with your spouse-to-be?

2. Think of friends of yours who have gotten married. What changed in your relationships with them when they got married?

3. If you've been married, what changes did you notice in your relationships with each other, your families, friends, and with the wider world when you got married?

4. Whether or not you've ever been married, what does marriage— as opposed to living together and promising commitment to each other—mean to you now? Are there aspects of marriage that scare you?

CHAPTER 11

SEX, GOOD SEX, AND SACRED SEX

I'm assuming you might be interested in this chapter for one of three reasons.

Reason number one: your sex life is somehow unsatisfactory. Maybe it's nonexistent, or you want it more than your partner does, or your partner wants it more than you do. Maybe you're both interested but it just isn't very good, or you're having problems becoming aroused, staying aroused, or otherwise performing the way you wish you could. You're looking for some help to make it better.

Reason number two: Your sex life is basically good and you're happy with your partner, but you're curious about how it might be enhanced further, as a pathway to growth and greater fulfillment. And something about that idea of "sacred sex" in the chapter title caught your attention.

Reason number three: it's a chapter talking about sex. And even though you've already figured out that this is not pornography, maybe there's something here that you'll find, well, sexy!

Of course, you might be interested in this chapter for some combination of those reasons, or some other reason altogether. But I'm assuming it's pretty much one of those three. Sex is important to you, whether you're having problems with it, you'd like to enhance your experience of it, or you're just excited by thinking about it. Any of those are good reasons to be reading this chapter.

So—let's talk about sex.

As the title of the chapter implies, I'm going to talk about three types: plain old sex, good sex, and sacred sex. As you'll see, they overlap, but they aren't the same. And as far as a course in sex goes, this one is cumulative: to have good sex, you'll need to have mastered the basics of plain old sex, and to have sacred sex, you have to be well versed in good sex.

Plain Old Sex

The first type, plain old sex, is pretty much what you probably think it is, in a broad sense. Plain old sex can include sex by yourself, or all sorts of sexual activities with others—we're not just talking about intercourse.

Most people want sex, or at least they did at some point. Physiologically, most of us are wired to seek it out, just like we do with other appetites, like hunger and thirst. It usually feels good on a basic level when that appetite is satisfied.

However, unlike hunger and thirst, our desire for sex is usually focused on others, and so it requires us to function socially. So sexual desire turns out to be a lot more complex, involving a mix of physiological, psychological, relational, and cultural factors.[64]

Like other generally pleasurable bodily activities, people experience plain old sex in a lot of different ways: as fun and relaxation, as a distraction from anxieties, or even as an addictive compulsion.

And, like other bodily activities, sex can happen in abusive contexts. My main focus in this chapter is on sex that involves consenting, autonomous adults. But I do need to mention sex in non-consenting contexts because it's unfortunately common, and it's often a big factor in the problems brought to me by couples. Perhaps you have experienced rape, molestation, or other sexual violations, and you're wondering if you can have—or perhaps regain—the healthy sexuality that was injured by that abuse. The short answer is yes, you can. But, as we discussed in Chapter 5, it might take some work in therapy to help you get there.

---

[64] The physiological factors, of course, are the domain of physicians, not psychologists; I won't be addressing those in this book. But if you're experiencing difficulties in your sex life, be it lack of interest in sex, pain during intercourse, trouble getting or staying aroused, or other body-related problems, checking with a physician could be just what you need. The one caveat I would offer is that you find a physician who understands that sexual issues are often multidimensional—it's not just about hormones or plumbing. Of course, that's equally true of finding a psychotherapist—it's not just about psychology!

Even if you haven't been traumatized in some specific way, you might still feel that sex is scary, or somehow wrong, dirty, or shameful. There are all sorts of sources from which you might have absorbed those messages: from your parents, either by explicit teaching or implicit example; from your peers; from the media, religious leaders, teachers, and other cultural influences; or even just from difficult personal experiences.

Those negative feelings about sex and sexual pleasure are a problem even for plain old sex, to say nothing of good sex or sacred sex. The premise of this chapter is that sex—even plain old sex—is a positive, healthy, potentially joyous part of living. If you don't feel that way, but wish you could, therapy might help.

But whether or not you get help from a therapist, there are some basic skills you need for plain old sex. Here are some questions to help you find the areas that might need work.

First, how do you feel about giving yourself physical pleasure? Is it okay to masturbate to orgasm? If you aren't okay with giving yourself sexual pleasure, why aren't you? Were you told it was wrong, or dirty, or that it would cause illness?

I'm not trying to imply that you need to masturbate to be healthy. People choose to abstain from sexual activity in general, or masturbation in particular, for all sorts of reasons, including medical issues, religious or philosophical beliefs, or simple lack of interest. That's not pathological. And of course, some people need to abstain from masturbating because the practice has become problematic— perhaps as part of an addictive pattern, an obsessive-compulsive ritual, or as a way of avoiding intimacy with a partner.

If you want to improve your sex life, but the thought of masturbation causes you anxiety, you need to start by getting in touch—literally and figuratively—with your own sexuality. You'll need to learn, by experience, that sexual pleasure can feel good and isn't dangerous. You'll need to develop the capacity to stay emotionally present during sex, and to feel whatever you feel—two skills that are often compromised by a history of abuse. And while you're at it, you can learn more about your own body and your own sexual likes and dislikes. If you need help with these things, get yourself to a therapist who is comfortable talking about sex.

If you're okay with sex with yourself, how do you feel about sex with a partner? Is it okay to receive pleasure from a partner? Is it okay to give pleasure to a partner? Can you share sexual pleasure with a partner you love, or does it have to be someone you're not too bonded with? Can you see your partner as both someone you desire sexually and someone you love emotionally and spiritually? If you feel that sex is somehow dirty or shameful—or worse, that you yourself are somehow dirty or shameful—you'll have a difficult time desiring someone whom you love and respect, or expecting to be loved and respected by a sexual partner. Again, working with a therapist can help you heal from the pain that such messages may have caused you, so you can experience sex with a partner as positive and loving.

Another question about sex with a partner: do you feel able to say no, even at the risk of disappointing your partner? If you can't say no, you can't really say yes. If you're in an abusive relationship, you need to get out and get safe. But even if your partner isn't abusive, you might still be afraid to say no because you've come to believe that giving yourself to them sexually is the only way you'll be lovable. This is often another consequence of sexual abuse, or harmful messages from earlier in your life. And if you're afraid to say no because you don't ever want to hurt or disappoint your partner, regardless of your own feelings or preferences, then you're essentially shutting off part of who you are—which is the opposite of intimacy. You can have sex that way, but not good sex or sacred sex. Again, if that's you, get yourself to a therapist and work on learning to say no when you need to.

And one more thing about plain old sex: to have sex with a partner—even to have sex with yourself, for that matter—you also need to have some basic understanding of anatomy (what's where) and physiology (what does what). You'd be amazed—or maybe you wouldn't—at how many otherwise well-educated people have such little knowledge of how their own body works, to say nothing of how their partner's body works. If you realize that this is you, some basic sex education might also be helpful.

Okay, so let's say you view sex positively, are comfortable with your own body, and have a pretty good idea of how everything works and what feels good. Congratulations! You're ready to move from plain old sex to good sex.

Good Sex

What is good sex, and how do you make it happen?

Plain old sex becomes good sex when you can be fully present and fully alive. If plain old sex is a physical way of connecting, good sex is a physical way of connecting intimately—and intimacy is the medium of growth. What I mean by good sex, then, is sex that does more than just fulfill a need or provide pleasure. Good sex helps you become more of who you are; it's about growth.

To have good sex, you need to be open to learning, open to guidance, and willing to take risks. You need to develop your capacity for passion, desire, and intimacy, which requires the maturity to take responsibility for your own feelings. And to have good sex, you must also develop radical respect for your partner's ability and need to do the same.

Essentially, you can develop the capacity for good sex once you can tolerate the anxiety that comes with it. Of course, the premise that intimacy requires you to tolerate anxiety is pretty much what Part II of this book is about. What, specifically, does tolerating anxiety have to do with good sex? Everything—well, three things, anyway.

First, for sex to become good sex, you have to let yourself know what you do and don't want, and communicate that to your partner, as well as listen to what your partner does or doesn't want. And sometimes, that's scary. Can you let yourself know what you like? And act on it? Can you handle it when your partner does the same? Can you stay present and open when your partner tells you they want you to do something differently, or do you feel rejected and hurt? If you can't receive the gift of actual honesty, then you can't have good sex.

Second, for sex to become good, you must be willing to expand your skill set past the limits of the predictable and comfortable. And, by definition, that means considering things that might make you anxious (at least at first). You might need to consider techniques or positions that you've been afraid to try. But most importantly, you must listen to your own and your partner's desires with an open mind.

Does the thought of sharing a hidden desire with your partner, or hearing about your partner's desire that you didn't know about, make you anxious? Probably! And over time, many couples avoid that anxiety and find their sexual repertoire reduced down to a predictable routine. It's comfortable, but it's deadly. To feel alive means to risk new experiences, and that means tolerating anxiety.

Of course, you shouldn't force yourself or let yourself be coerced into doing things you don't want to do. In fact, that would be the very opposite of listening to your own desires—it would be shutting part of yourself down. Rather, expanding your skill set means opening yourself to learning—learning from your partner, learning from your own experiences (both positive and negative), and from reading, conversation, and any and all other sources. To be open to learning means you can tolerate the anxiety of having your beliefs and even your values challenged; it also means you're willing to learn from failure, as well as success. You might try something and find you just don't like it. But if you don't try, you won't expand your skills, and that's a recipe for a dying sexual relationship. Conversely, when you risk learning new skills, your sexual relationship is continually renewed.

The third factor that might cause you anxiety on your way to good sex involves the inevitable differences between you and your partner—differences in preference, differences in desire, differences in how you handle the stresses between you—all sorts of differences that exist simply because you're two different people.

In particular, how you handle it when one of you wants sex and the other doesn't is a great indicator of whether or not you're capable of good sex. In fact, how you handle this particular problem is not only an indicator, it's also a causal factor in whether or not you're capable of good sex.

Because no matter how sophisticated your sexual technique, if you can't handle that particular disappointment with grace and generosity, you'll have a hard time with other differences, too. Like when one of you tells the other you've always wanted to try role playing, or toys, or some particular technique, and the other is repulsed by the fantasy. Or when it just doesn't work for one of you—you don't stay aroused, can't seem to reach orgasm, or just aren't feeling it.

These situations can either be turned into opportunities for grace and caring, or into triggers of resentment and recrimination. The outcome depends on whether or not you can tolerate the anxiety of being out of sync with your partner.[65] If the hardness of his penis or the wetness of her vagina become indices of whether your partner loves you, desires you, or respects you—or even worse, if they become indices of your own desirability in general—then you're enacting a cycle that leads to sexual death.[66] But if you're able to handle the anxiety, to soothe yourself and stay present, those apparent problems are just opportunities for compassion, creativity, and deeper bonding.

And that's one of the ironies of good sex: sometimes, the greatest thing for your sex life is when something goes wrong, because problems are what push you to grow. If you can't tolerate the anxiety and stay present when things go wrong, you can't have good sex.

David Schnarch, who has written extensively about sexual connection in committed couples, points out that problems related to desire are not only possible in a long-term relationship, but inevitable, "part of the normal, healthy processes of marriage" (Schnarch, 2011). As we discussed in Chapter 4, our efforts to avoid anxiety for the sake of stability tend to result in a loss of intimacy, and that can lead to sexual problems.

Just as therapy can help you get past the triggers, fears, and beliefs that interfere with even plain old sex, it can also teach you how to handle anxiety, so as to make good sex possible. And good sex, as you probably realize, isn't just about sex: to be capable of good sex is to be capable of intimate connection in other ways as well, even in non-sexual relationships. When couples consult me for therapy, we often find that working on their sexual connection improves their ability to connect in other ways, and vice versa.

Which brings us to the third part of this chapter: sacred sex.

Sacred Sex

Plain old sex is a physical way of connecting; good sex is a physical way of connecting intimately. So what's sacred sex?

Like good sex, sacred sex is a physical expression of intimate

---

[65]See Chapter 6.

[66]A recent article (Dickson, 2018) describes the stigma associated with lubricants—for heterosexual people in particular—reflecting "a common misconception: that lube indicates a less than healthy sex life." That belief itself is a setup for sex problems.

connection, but it's also more than that. The word "sacred" means something set apart from the everyday, something dedicated to a higher purpose. Sacred sex, then, means sex that is elevated, dedicated to something beyond ordinary connection.

Sacred sex doesn't just connect you to yourself or your partner—it connects you to the essence of all being. In Western religious terms, sacred sex connects you to God. In Eastern traditions such as tantra, sacred sex implies the release of spiritual energies that connect you to greater realities. Even in secular terms, sacred sex is an experience of transcendence: you experience the reality that you are part of the whole, a participant in the ongoing creation of all that is.

What is it about sex that makes sacred sex possible, more than, say, sacred dishwashing or sacred ditch-digging? Of course, many traditions would say that both of those are possible, too, because pretty much anything we do can be elevated to a higher meaning. But sex is particularly suited to the experience of the sacred precisely because the forces involved in sex—specifically in good sex—are so conducive to taking you out of your own narrow experience.

To experience the sacred is to be awe-struck, to experience a power much greater than yourself, which can be both thrilling and terrifying. Think back to your first experience of orgasm, assuming you've experienced it. Whether it felt good, bad, or some combination of the two, you probably found that the sheer power of orgasm is itself awesome. It's the ability of sex to inspire awe that makes sacred sex possible, if you can be open to the experience.

How do you open yourself to the experience of sacred sex? Curiously, it's not about learning techniques for mind-blowing orgasms, though such techniques can certainly enhance good sex. Rather, opening yourself to sacred sex is more about the sacred than about the sex. Developing the capacity for sacred sex means being able to experience the sacred in all aspects of your life. It's when you find sacredness in everyday things that the power of sex to evoke sacredness can emerge; and that means cultivating faith.

As we discussed in Part III, faith is when you accept that reality is right—not merely real, but right—even when it's difficult, even when you can't understand it, even when you want to change it. Faith is how you open yourself up to experiencing sacredness, because accepting the rightness of reality can transform terror into awe, anxiety into acceptance, and frozen despair into active determination. When you experience your own existence as part of something much bigger, you can recognize the sacredness all around you.[67]

And that's when you can experience the intimacy of good sex as something much more than pleasure and satisfaction. When you are open to sacredness, good sex can be elevated to an experience of cosmic creativity, in which your physical and emotional sensations connect you to a deeper sense of meaning and fulfillment.

The Chasidic Rabbi Simcha Bunim of Peshischa said that everyone should carry around two slips of paper, each expressing a vital truth. When you're feeling depressed, pull out the slip that says, "The universe was created for my sake." When you're feeling arrogant and full of yourself, pull out the slip that says, "I am but dust and ashes."

Sacred sex invites us to experience those two truths simultaneously. We are physical beings—dust and ashes—driven by powerful forces to have sex, and we can do so thoughtlessly or mindfully, cruelly or lovingly, clumsily or skillfully. And we are also capable of self-awareness, which makes us feel in awe at our place in the universe and can transform sex into an experience of sacredness.

Plain old sex, good sex, and sacred sex are all expressions of who we are and who we can become. More than just the satisfaction of a physical urge, sex can be a source of connection, intimacy, and meaning. Developing and practicing faith is the key.

Reflections:
Sex, Good Sex, and Sacred Sex

1. How did you learn about sex? What kind of messages did you get from parents, other adults, and peers about sex?

2. How well do you know your own sexual anatomy and physiology? How well do you know your sexual likes and dislikes?

3. If you have a partner, how well do you know your partner's body

---

[67]Note the parallel with marriage, as we discussed in Chapter 10. Marriage connects a relationship to something bigger. Sacred sex does the same for good sex.

and preferences? How well does your partner know your body and preferences? Are you able to talk with your partner about sex? Do you feel free to decline sex with your partner? Do you feel free to initiate sex?

4. How do you distinguish between plain old sex and good sex in your own experience?

5. Have you ever experienced sacredness, sexually or otherwise? What felt sacred to you? How do you know when you're in the presence of the sacred?

CHAPTER 12

INFIDELITY

Infidelity is not rare. In the United States, data from the General Social Survey from NORC at the University of Chicago show that among people who have been married, about 20 percent of men and 13 percent of women reported having had sex with someone besides their spouse while they were married.[68] One site (Truth About Deception, 2019) reported estimates that "roughly 30 to 60 percent of all married individuals (in the United States) will engage in infidelity at some point during their marriage," and that 2 to 3 percent of all children are the product of infidelity, mostly without the knowledge of the men who raised them. Esther Perel, in her book *The State of Affairs (2017)*, mentions prevalence rates of 26 to 70 percent for women and 33 to 75 percent for men. Of course, what people are willing to report, and what they consider "having sex," will affect survey results dramatically, as reflected by the large ranges of the various estimates.

But any way you define it, infidelity is common. You know people who have cheated, and people who have been affected by cheating. You yourself might be in either or both of those categories. I don't know the exact proportion in my practice, but I'd estimate about a third of the couples I see are dealing with the effects of infidelity of one kind or another; I've seen hundreds of couples dealing with it.

In this chapter we'll consider five guidelines that I've found helpful for couples as they work to heal from infidelity. Some of the guidelines are particularly relevant for the partner who's been cheated on, and some for the partner who cheated, but whichever role you might be in, it's helpful to understand the other.[69]

---

[68] I based this estimate on data aggregated from GSS surveys between 2002 and 2016 (NORC, 2018).

[69] I'll be using the terms "cheated on" and "cheater" as shorthand for those roles. I realize the term "cheater" sounds harsh, but am willing to risk that for the sake of simplicity. In my experience, the couples who are dealing with infidelity are clear about who's who, and we don't avoid the labels. Of course, I've seen couples where both partners are in both roles.

What Does Healing from Infidelity Look Like?

Before we get to those five guidelines, let's consider what healing from infidelity might look like. Since infidelity (and especially its discovery) is a traumatic event for each partner and the couple as an entity, we can apply the ideas we discussed in Chapter 5 about healing from trauma. You know you've healed from trauma when reminders of the event evoke memories without triggering emergency responses. When you encounter something you associate with the traumatic event (consciously or unconsciously) and your response is no longer dominated by fight, flight, or freeze, you've healed.

For each of you, that means that you've healed once you're no longer thrown into panic when you're reminded of the infidelity. And for the two of you as a couple, that means you don't dissolve into arguments or frozen silence when the topic comes up.

Healing implies forgiveness. As we discussed in Chapter 9, forgiveness does not mean you'll restore trust (recall that you can forgive someone without trusting them at all), or that you'll necessarily stay together. Forgiveness certainly doesn't mean minimizing the pain or justifying immorality; it's not denying that what they did was hurtful and wrong.

Rather, forgiveness means you can let go of the anger. Whether you stay together or not, healing means you're free from the panic. If you split up but must stay in contact—for example, if you have kids together—then forgiveness is a vital goal, because you don't want your interactions to be dominated by anger.

Forgiveness can feel a very long way off when you're first confronted with infidelity. If you've just discovered your partner's infidelity, you may feel hurt, shocked, betrayed, and many other confusing and painful emotions. It feels like your world is coming apart. If you're the one who's been caught cheating, you're dealing with a lot of those same emotions, often accompanied by large doses of both guilt and shame.[70] You can

---

[70] If you're the cheater and you feel neither guilt nor shame, you won't get much out of this chapter, or this book. But, as we'll discuss, that doesn't mean you should be stuck in either guilt or shame. Your healing work will eventually involve forgiving yourself.

heal, but it will take work. And it won't be comfortable, regardless of whether or not you want to stay with your partner.

But, as many couples have assured me, healing is worth the effort. In fact, many people have expressed gratitude, not for the cheating itself, but for the crisis that forced them into growth. Whatever the outcome, in terms of your relationship's future, you'll both grow from the experience.

If you're near the beginning of your healing journey—that is, if you've just found out about the cheating or been caught doing it—the idea that you'll grow from the experience can seem remote to the point of absurdity. It's hard to appreciate panic! But knowing that one day you'll appreciate the growth reflects an attitude of faith. You probably won't notice it right away, but, as we've discussed, faith is what keeps you from panicking. Just knowing that it will get better, that you'll find a way to work with the reality of the situation—even though you don't know how yet—is what will get you through that initial period of shock and grief. The fact that you're reading this book implies that you're hopeful, at least, that you can get through this. You're already showing faith.

That's the sort of healing that you're working toward: you'll not only feel released from the anger, but you'll be able to appreciate the pain as a meaningful growth experience. How do you get there? Let's consider five guidelines.

Guideline #1: Check Your Assumptions

Perhaps you've noticed that I haven't defined just what constitutes infidelity. That's because each of us has our own assumptions of what's okay and what isn't, and we're not always conscious of how we feel until something comes up to challenge those assumptions.

Most couples I've worked with have agreed on monogamy, but it's not always clear what that means.[71] Most of the time, it means they expect each other to refrain from sexual intercourse with anyone else,

---

[71]Even couples who practice some form of polyamory, do threesomes, or go to BDSM, swinging, or other sex-oriented conventions deal with infidelity when someone violates their shared understanding of the rules. And the pain feels just as intense.

and usually they consider other forms of in-person genital contact, penetrative or not, to be out of bounds as well.[72] I'm guessing that's true for most (though not all) of you reading this book.

But there are all sorts of variations that aren't as clear, especially since the internet has made available forms of interaction that never existed before. Is masturbating while video chatting with a live person cheating? There are now devices available that allow someone to control a sex toy remotely. Is that cheating? What about sex with an interactive video or robot? Or just sex with an inflatable doll? Or rubber genitalia? Is looking at pornography cheating? Is masturbation itself cheating, even without pornography? What about just thinking of some other person's body while having sex with your partner?

And what about non-sexual cheating, what people often call an emotional affair? When does a close friendship cross into forbidden territory?

Not only are the variations endless, but what each of us considers cheating can change with time and circumstance. Attitudes can change with experience.

When you find yourself reacting with horror to something your partner has done, or something you think they've done, check your assumptions. Could you be wrong about what happened? Is it something you don't *have* to think of as cheating, even if it's distasteful to you? This doesn't mean you should be okay with behavior that violates your values; it mean that you need to understand that there are degrees of wrong. You might object to your partner's looking at porn, for example, but recognize that it's not as much of a betrayal as an affair with someone. If you can't make that distinction, you're going to have a much harder time. And if you can't imagine that your partner could ever have a stray thought, you're deluding yourself. Whatever your partner did, you need to confront your own judgments about it and be clear with yourself about what's important to you. Your partner isn't the embodiment of evil, even though they may have done things that are morally wrong.

---

[72]I've met many people—almost all men—who consider anonymous hookups (paid or unpaid) as *not* cheating, but feel that sex as part of a personal relationship *is* cheating. Typically, they're in my office talking about it because their partner doesn't make that distinction. I also recognize that a large majority of the couples I see are heterosexual, as am I, and so I am used to heteronormative rules and preferences. As I mentioned in the introduction, the examples I've used in this book are based on that experience. But for any couple, gay or straight, when infidelity is an issue I don't assume any particular definitions of fidelity or cheating; I ask what they mean to the couple.

You need to have some perspective, and you can't do that unless you calm down and get hold of yourself. Take some time for this.

Somewhere along the way you'll need to consider your own role in how your relationship got to where it is, rather than assuming that the crisis is entirely about your partner. That does not mean that you're responsible for your partner's cheating—you're not. However, it does mean that you'll benefit from taking responsibility for your own participation, not only in the past, but in the present as well. It's tempting to insist that your partner fix the relationship, since they broke it. But that's ultimately futile, and it will just leave you feeling powerless. If you decide that you no longer can stay with your partner, that's up to you; and if you decide that you want to try to restore trust, that's also up to you. It doesn't seem fair, but at some point, you'll have to make that decision, and blaming your partner for it will just leave you miserable.

If you're the one accused of cheating, you also need to check your assumptions. Of course, you could be genuinely taken aback by your partner's anger because you didn't think you were doing anything morally wrong, or violating any implicit or explicit agreement with your partner—maybe you don't think you cheated at all. If so, you'll do well to consider your partner's objections carefully and examine your own attitudes. If you listen with an open heart, you might come to understand how your actions were hurtful; alternatively, you might come to understand that you have a serious difference between you that needs to be hashed out in order for your relationship to continue. Either way, this is a great example of how important it is to get to the right argument, as we discussed in Chapter 6.

More commonly in my experiences with couples, the one accused of cheating agrees that they cheated. They may have denied it at first, but by the time the couple makes an appointment to see me, the one who cheated has usually admitted at least some of it—otherwise, it's rare that the cheater is willing to come.

If you've admitted to cheating, you need to look carefully at how your assumptions are shaping your reactions. You're probably feeling a mix of shame at being caught, guilt because you violated your own values, fear about your future, and some built-up resentment that helped justify your cheating in the first place.

If you're the cheater, you'll need to confront the assumption that you're a bad person, which is what shame is trying to convince you. You're not a bad person; you did a bad thing. In order to heal, you must accept your basic validity—that is, overcome the shame—so you can experience the appropriate guilt and get hold of yourself enough to clean up the mess as best you can. As we discussed in Chapter 6, if you're dominated by shame, your focus will be on what others think of you, especially your partner. When you get past shame and experience guilt, your focus will be on doing the right thing, according to your own moral compass.

You'll also need to confront the assumption that your partner owes you forgiveness. Even if you've been very apologetic and offered sufficient assurances of good behavior, assuming that your partner owes you forgiveness can turn out to be one of the greatest pitfalls to actually gaining forgiveness. You may not be aware that you're assuming it—that is, you might intellectually believe and profess otherwise. But if you've ever angrily told your partner to just "move on" and get over it already, that's precisely what you're assuming, whether you recognize it consciously or not. Without that assumption, you might wish your partner would get over it, and be sad that they haven't, but you wouldn't be angry about their lack of forgiveness. You're only angry at your partner for not doing something when you feel entitled to it. And feeling entitled to forgiveness won't encourage your partner to offer it—on the contrary, it tends to keep them angry.

Whichever role you're in, be prepared to check your assumptions. You may find that you'll change some long-held beliefs, or you may find that you'll clarify and strengthen those beliefs. But either way, you'll have a better sense of who you are, with less panic.

Guideline #2: You Don't Need All the Details

This guideline is primarily for the cheated-on partner, though it can help inform the cheater as well.

Remember John and Millie from Chapter 9? Millie had been texting with an old boyfriend, and John had discovered it. When they came to see me, Millie had already broken off the (digital) relationship with the old boyfriend and given John access to her phone whenever he wanted to check it. She assured him that he had seen all the texts they had exchanged, and she endured seemingly endless interrogation about exactly what every text meant to her. Any time John was reminded of what Millie had done—for example, when a TV drama included infidelity in its plot—he would think of possible interpretations that he hadn't considered and demand an explanation from Millie.

What John thought he needed—what many people in his situation think they need—was something from his partner that would settle his anxiety, one way or the other. If Millie could just say the right words, he'd either feel better and get back to the way things were, or have his worst fears confirmed and realize he needs to break up and move on. Either way, he'd be out of the purgatory of uncertainty. And Millie felt guilty enough that she was willing to put up with his demands, because she too was focused on getting back to how things were before.

That's what John thought he needed and what Millie wanted to provide: reassurance so they could go back to being okay.

But what you actually need if you're the cheated-on partner isn't constant reassurance; rather, what you need is to make sense of the situation so you can decide what to do about your relationship.

When you first discovered you'd been betrayed, you probably felt shock and disbelief, followed by a mix of anger, sadness, and fear about your future. But as you are able to accept the realities of what happened, and get past panic mode, you form a new understanding of your situation. It's a painful process, involving a reevaluation of your partner, yourself, and your relationship. Whatever you decide to do about the relationship—stay or leave—your understanding won't be the same as it was before the betrayal. If your relationship survives, it will be based on a new, richer understanding of how you got to where you are. You won't get back to the way things were—which is a good thing, since the way things were is what brought you to the betrayal.

Now it's true that you do need some information from the cheater in order to accept the realities of the situation. You need to know that your suspicions (if, like most people, you had some) turned out to be well-founded, that you weren't paranoid.

But that common tendency to want more and more details about the infidelity doesn't serve you well. That urge is coming from part of you that doesn't want to believe the infidelity actually happened. As I mentioned in Chapter 9, many of our mental processes have no sense of time. Those time-blind parts of you feel that maybe if your partner says the right thing, or you just keep looking at the evidence, you'll magically realize that it was all a bad dream. But pressing for more and more details won't help—because it did in fact happen. You're going to have to accept that reality, and nothing your partner says will take it away. Your partner probably already tried to do that by lying or minimizing when you first discovered the infidelity. It didn't work then, and it won't work now.

Essentially, if you found out your partner was having sex with someone else, you don't need to know what positions they used. Don't go there. Your dignity is more important.

What if you're the cheater, and your offended partner won't stop pressing you for details? You might be tempted to quote this guideline to your partner, in hopes that they'll back off. Well, don't! You're in no position to determine what's right for your partner as they struggle to make sense of what you did. Any advice you offer your partner is hopelessly compromised by a conflict of interest. Your efforts to control your partner's healing process will backfire.

However, the fact that your partner is asking you questions doesn't mean you have to answer them. I offer this as an observation, not an opinion—I'm not saying what you should or shouldn't do in a given moment. I'm just observing that you can make your own choices about what you say, even if your partner is demanding answers.

You'll probably want to err on the side of more, rather than less disclosure if you want your partner to stay with you. But the point is that you're responsible for what you choose to talk about. If you feel you're being hounded by your partner, you can choose to not answer. Recognize, of course, that the consequence might be the end of the relationship. But it's an option. And, if you do choose to answer your partner's questions, don't blame your partner for your choice.

For that matter, you could choose to lie or minimize, as you almost certainly did during and after the infidelity.[73] Here the guideline is simple: don't.

---

[73]Or perhaps you're one of the rare exceptions who told the full truth as soon as your infidelity was discovered. I've met such people, but not many, and even then they were deceiving their partner by omission while they were carrying on the infidelity.

Guideline #3: Monitoring Your Partner Won't Help You Rebuild Trust

If your partner still wants to cheat, they can cheat, no matter how much you check their iPhone. Making yourself their probation officer is no basis for an intimate relationship. The hard fact is that you're going to have to decide whether you trust them enough to stay. You'll have to decide if the cheating was a symptom of something that the two of you can fix, or an indication that you need to move on. It might take you some time to know.

Yes, your monitoring might uncover further evidence of cheating, and if so, you can decide it's over. But what if you don't find more evidence? If you're still uncertain, you'll keep monitoring, and it will just cause more damage to your relationship. Ultimately, the one you need to trust is yourself—not that you can ever be absolutely certain your partner won't cheat again, but that you'd be able to deal with it if it happened. The hard work is confronting your self-doubt and self-blame. No amount of detective work will help you with that.

If you're the cheater, this guideline is similar to the previous one. You won't get anywhere trying to convince your partner not to be your probation officer. But you'll have to decide for yourself what to go along with, and what to (respectfully) decline to disclose. It's unlikely you'll want to stay in a relationship where your partner insists on tracking your every move. If you do say no to monitoring, it could cost you the relationship—or it could be just what your relationship needs to heal. There's no easy formula, which is an unfortunate consequence of deceiving your partner.

Even if you decline to be monitored, don't lie about what you've been up to. You could say no to monitoring, but don't make up innocent-sounding responses just to avoid your partner's suspicions.

Guideline #4: Be Your Best Self, Not Your Worst

This guideline, of course, applies to everyone. But it's particularly relevant if you've been cheated on. You might be tempted to punish your offending partner. I've met cheated-on partners who have become so consumed by righteous indignation that they actively looked for opportunities to humiliate and debase their partner, sometimes justifying it as a way to teach their partner how it feels.

Punishing your partner won't help you feel better—even if it does temporarily, it will come back to hurt you later. You're not the embodiment of pure good any more than your partner is the embodiment of pure evil. You're both human, so hold your head up. Control your anger. Be a grown-up. Yes, it hurts. You are still responsible for how you handle it.

Guideline #5: Forgiveness is Up to You

We talked earlier in this chapter about what healing from infidelity looks like. Eventually, you'll each want to free yourself from anger, shame, and guilt, and come to see the infidelity as a painful but important learning experience. That process of freeing yourself from traumatic effects and seeing the situation with a mature perspective is what I've referred to in this book as forgiveness.

If you're the one who was cheated on, some well-meaning friends, family members, clergy, or other professionals might push you to forgive your partner. You could even interpret my emphasis on forgiveness in this chapter as pressure to forgive. After all, if forgiveness means freedom from a lot of painful emotions, why not forgive?

I do think you'll be better off, eventually, when you can forgive. But you can't forgive until you're ready, and no one can determine that timing for you. As we discussed in Chapter 9, if you're still in the acute phase of being hurt in the relationship, anger might be your protective response, and you might need it for a while. You are, of course, still responsible for how you express your anger (see Guideline #4 above), but you may still need to feel it, and to distance yourself from your partner as necessary.

In particular, the cheater's understandable desire for your forgiveness doesn't mean you can offer it before you're ready. Remember that your forgiveness isn't about the cheater, or whether or not they deserve forgiveness. Indeed, you could forgive the cheater regardless of whether or not they deserve it, and regardless of whether or not you trust them enough to stay in the relationship. Forgiveness is about your own readiness to let go of the hurt. That will almost certainly take a lot longer than the cheater wishes it would. Don't be spiteful, but your partner's desire for forgiveness isn't your problem.

If you're the cheater, reread the previous paragraph. Your partner's forgiveness isn't about you. Instead, in order to repair the relationships you've damaged, you'll need to work on forgiving yourself.

The five guidelines we've discussed in this chapter can be quite helpful as you work toward healing. But the work will be painful whether you adhere to them or not, and it will undoubtedly take longer than you would hope.[74]

Adhering to the guidelines can help you get hold of yourself—or maybe it would be more accurate to say, if you get hold of yourself, you'll be able to adhere to the guidelines. To follow these guidelines is to embody faith, the acceptance that reality is fundamentally right even when it hurts. However you and your partner emerge from the crisis, together or separate, you'll find meaning in what you've gone through. You'll grow.

Reflections: Infidelity

1. How do you define infidelity in your own relationship with a partner? Has your definition changed over time? If you have a partner, do you think they share your definition? Have you talked about it explicitly?

2. Have you ever been cheated on by a partner? How did you handle it in terms of the five guidelines of this chapter?

3. Have you ever been caught cheating on a partner? How did you handle it in terms of the five guidelines of this chapter?

---

[74]To paraphrase D.C. Jarvis (1958) from his book *Folk Medicine*: If you use Vermont folk medicine, you'll get over your cold in a week. If not, it'll take seven days.

CHAPTER 13

HOW DO YOU KNOW WHEN TO CALL IT QUITS?

When a couple decides to seek therapy, as I mentioned in Chapter 1, they've often been dealing with serious issues for a long time. If that's your situation, you may well be wondering when it's time to call it quits on a relationship. Something hurts—a lot—and it's gotten to the point that you're wondering if you should stay in the relationship or break up. So how do you decide?

Deal-Breakers versus Growing Pains

Let's divide your problems into two categories: we'll call them deal-breakers and growing pains. If you're looking at deal-breakers, the thing to do is, well, break the deal. If you're looking at growing pains, don't break up—at least not yet. Rather, tolerate the pain and grow through it.

Okay, all we've done is name the dilemma. How can you tell which problems are which kind?

Let's start with deal-breakers. You want to have kids, and your partner doesn't. If you're a woman wanting to get pregnant, the clock is ticking. Or perhaps you want to get married, and your partner doesn't, or vice versa. Or it turns out that one of you is gay, the other straight, and sex in your relationship is important to you. Or you're religiously observant, and your partner objects, and you don't know how you could have children together unless you were united on that issue. Or you realize you can't bear living in the city, and your partner can't bear living anywhere else but the city. Or you can't imagine living without your cat, and your partner can't stand cats.

The thing about deal-breakers is that compromise isn't possible. You can't both have and not have kids. If it's a deal-breaker, it's difficult, but it's not complicated. You know what the problem is. You just have to decide if you can give up what you want or convince your partner to give up what they want. If not, it won't work.

But most of the problems people talk about when they work with me are not so simple. These are the problems in the other category: growing pains.

You used to have a warm connection with your partner, emotionally and physically, but now it seems like you dread being in your partner's presence. Or you find yourself attracted to someone else, or your partner does, and maybe one of you acted on it.[75] Or you find out that your partner has lied to you about something important. Or you just can't seem to talk with each other about your sex life, your finances, issues about your kids, or your concerns about your partner's substance use without it turning into a fight. Or you feel you're somehow with the wrong partner, but you've built a life together and you can't imagine losing what you've built.

These situations aren't necessarily deal-breakers, because you might be able to find each other again, rebuild trust, make changes, and feel good about staying together. It's not like there's no possible solution, at least in theory; but if you've been struggling with it and nothing has worked, it sure can seem that way.

When couples come to my office, it's often as a last resort: either they find some hope that they can make it work, or it's over. But how can you tell if you should keep some hope for the relationship?

There's no simple formula. But here are three guidelines to help you.

Guideline #1: Don't Break Up Too Soon

Assuming your personal safety isn't at risk, your struggles are forcing you to grow. If you leave before you've learned what you need to learn, you'll probably have to go through it again with someone else.

Of course, only you can determine what's too soon. But there are

---

[75]See Chapter 12.

some particularly bad reasons that often lead people to break up too early.

If you think you'll do better with the person who's waiting in the wings, you probably won't. That's not to say that you can't find a better relationship—but if you're looking for stability and intimacy,[76] breaking up with a committed partner to be with an affair partner is a recipe for disaster. You've been avoiding intimacy with one, and stability with the other. Unless you develop the skills to have both stability and intimacy, you'll probably have neither.[77] That's where the phenomenon of the "rebound relationship" gets its bad reputation.

If you want to stay together but your partner is unsure, you might find yourself feeling powerless—you can't make your partner want you, and your efforts to do so just seem to push them farther away. It might seem like the only power you have to change the situation is to call it quits. But if you break up out of despair or anger because you can't tolerate the anxiety of not being in control, you're still not getting what you want, and you'll just end up hurting yourself.

That's not to say that you should wait forever—you won't, and you shouldn't. But don't break up until you can do so both responsibly and accountably. Responsibly means that you're not blaming your partner for your own decision; accountably means you're doing so in a way that reflects respect for your obligations and moral values. You'll need to be free of panic—or at least enough that you're able to think clearly about what you really want.

That idea—that you need to get past panic so you can be clear about what you want—brings us to the second guideline.

Guideline #2: Get Hold of Yourself

Getting hold of yourself means tolerating anxiety, rather than trying to escape it. It's how you can manage the first guideline, to not break up too soon. When you recognize that anxiety comes with the territory of living, and especially with the territory of loving, you can stay present without dissolving into panic. Getting hold of yourself is what lets you get past anger and resentment so you can act responsibly

---

[76]If you checked out this chapter before reading Parts I through III, this would be a good time to start at the beginning of the book!

[77]Yes, I do know of occasional exceptions to this, and perhaps you do too. It's still a very bad bet.

and accountably, whether you ultimately decide to stay together or not.

An important aspect of getting hold of yourself is accepting that you won't always be in sync with your partner—and you need to be able to get hold of yourself even when your partner isn't able to. Part of this ability is recognizing your assumptions about who is entitled to what, and being prepared to question those assumptions.[78] You may discover that you're able to accommodate your partner generously, on the one hand, or that it's clear that you can't, on the other. But either way, getting hold of yourself is the key.

Which leads to the third guideline.

Guideline #3: Get to the Right Argument

Couples often have important, substantive differences that they need to work out. But differences are scary, so much so that couples will often argue endlessly about anything and everything *except* what they really need to argue about. You can usually tell when you get to the right argument, because even if the argument is painful, it stops being infantile. You stop squabbling and face whatever difference is between you with courage. Maybe you realize, sadly, that it's a deal-breaker. But many couples, if they can tolerate the anxiety of not having an immediate solution, discover that mutual understanding can lead to growth and change.

Getting to the right argument requires you to not panic—you need to get hold of yourself, even if the difference you're dealing with threatens the stability of your relationship. Essentially, getting to the right argument means you're capable of intimacy.

Perhaps it won't surprise you to discover that the three guidelines—don't break up too soon, get hold of yourself, and get to the right argument—can map pretty well onto the seven-word formula, "Be kind, don't panic, and have faith." Don't break up too soon means don't give up on your kinship too quickly—be kind (in the way we discussed kindness in Part I); getting hold of yourself is all about not panicking (Part II); and the idea of getting to the right argument presupposes that there *is* a right argument—i.e., that even when it's painful and you don't have ready solutions, working to understand the

[78]See Chapter 6.

situation and each other will be meaningful. That's a statement of faith (Part III).

From that perspective, the decision about when to call it quits is just one example of the decisions you make every day in the course of any relationship. If you do so with kindness, clarity, and faith, you'll be able to cope with the inevitable uncertainties and live a life of meaning and purpose, even when you're faced with painful choices.

Reflections: How Do You Know When to Call It Quits?

1. Have you ever decided to break up with someone? If so, how did you come to the decision?

2. What are some deal-breakers for you? Have you ever decided to break up with someone because of a deal-breaker, even though you loved and respected the person? Has anyone broken up with you because of a deal-breaker?

3. Have you ever considered breaking up with someone because of growing pains (i.e., not clear deal-breakers), but worked through the problems and stayed together?

4. Have you ever considered breaking up with someone because of growing pains, worked on the problems, and still decided to break up? What did you learn from working on the problems, even though you didn't ultimately stay together?

CHAPTER 14

WHAT HAPPENED TO THOSE COUPLES?

You may have noticed that I haven't told you what happened to the couples we've met in this book. Did Patrick and Dierdre stay together or split up? What about Doris and Ken—did they get past the texting crisis? Did Trey and Tara find stability? I haven't finished any of their stories.

That's because, as I noted in the Introduction, all the couples are composites. Their stories are realistic, but not real; that is, they're all based on situations I've actually encountered in my practice, but the details have been changed to such an extent that there's no way anyone I've worked with could be identified as any of the couples. If you've worked with me, you might well recognize situations that are similar to your own, but I assure you you're not the couple in the book, because none of these situations was unique in my practice, and I made up the details. The couples I described here are not intended to represent any one couple that I've worked with.[79]

Therefore, I can't provide a definitive answer about any of the couples' fates. But let's see what *might* have happened to them, based on couples I've seen in similar situations.

Here they are, in order of appearance.

---

[79]On several occasions while writing this book, I informed couples I'd just met that I had recently written about a fictitious couple who were in a strikingly similar situation, to reassure them that the couple in the book isn't them.

Dierdre and Patrick

When we first encountered Dierdre and Patrick in Chapter 1, they were caught in a cycle of increasing resentment and misery, not caused by any one cataclysmic event like an affair, but by discontent that had been building up for years. Dierdre was irritated by pretty much anything Patrick did, much to her and Patrick's mutual consternation. And Patrick's attempts to repair the situation had become just more fodder for resentment. When they started therapy, Patrick was essentially convinced that this was Dierdre's problem to solve. Although she knew this couldn't be true, Dierdre was as distressed by her own apparently disproportionate anger as she was by anything Patrick did.

The fact that they hadn't split up already can be credited to more than just their shared kids, house, and finances. All of those factors were important, but it was also clear that their bond mattered to them. As our work progressed, Patrick began to realize how his own assumptions had shaped his attitudes toward Dierdre, and the effects this was having on their relationship. Once he saw that this wasn't only about Dierdre, he stopped responding to her as if it were. As Dierdre sensed that he was willing to hear her, she became less reactive and more honest—with both herself and Patrick—about what was important to her.

When we last heard from Dierdre and Patrick back in Chapter 6, they had begun to get hold of themselves and tolerate what was happening without panic. They were able to reestablish some emotional honesty with each other (also known as intimacy). They experienced fewer angry exchanges and had backed away from crisis mode.

So what happened next? Or, recalling that they're a fictitious couple, what has happened to couples like them?

In terms of the seven-word formula, Dierdre and Patrick are an illustration of what happens once a couple learns to not panic: as their reactivity softens, their sense of kinship can manifest again. They are able to be more kind.

Perhaps it turns out that Patrick and Dierdre, having gone to the edge of divorce, can now appreciate what they have in each other. That doesn't end their work, because the differences they've encountered are real and important; but it means they're prepared to face those differences without panic and find solutions together, whether in formal therapy or on their own.

Or, maybe one or the other—let's say Dierdre—realizes that she no longer wants to stay married, not because she's so miserable with Patrick, but because she's found a vital part of herself that can't thrive in the marriage. Even this won't end their work together, formally or otherwise, because breaking up a long marriage—especially with kids—is logistically and emotionally difficult. But their regained sense of kinship means that they can go through it with compassion and dignity.

Whatever the outcome, their ability to get hold of themselves and tolerate the anxiety of intimacy bodes well for each of them going forward.

Edgar and Sharon

If Dierdre and Patrick represented the loss of the assumption of good will, Edgar and Sharon might be an illustration of what happens when the assumption of good will goes too far. Recall that they had been referred to me by the psychiatric ward of the local hospital, where Sharon had spent a week after swallowing a handful of pills. Sharon's act of desperation took both of them by surprise, but as we talked about it in therapy, she described Edgar's frequent "poking fun" at the "stupid things" she does. She couldn't consciously interpret his actions as cruel, nor could he, because they both considered him a good husband. They both interpreted her reactions as evidence of her own weakness, and ultimately pathology.

What helped them out, as I described it in Chapter 1, may seem too simple—but I've experienced enough similar outcomes that the scenario is realistic. I told Edgar to just be nice—to listen to her, and not make fun of her. Sharon had been trying to get him to do that for decades, but until he almost lost her, he didn't hear it. And her experience of overdosing and ending up in the hospital, which marked her as a psychiatric patient and therefore of questionable sanity, didn't add to her credibility with Edgar. Sharon largely shared Edgar's opinion that this was her problem.

I generally avoid giving simplistic instructions to clients about how to behave (e.g., "be nice to her"). For me to tell another adult how to behave is arrogant—it implies that I know better than they do how they should live their lives. I'm happy to share my ideas and values—I'll tell people what I think might work and why. But my role as a therapist is to help people understand themselves and their situation so that *they* can decide how to behave, not to impose my own values on them by flat-out telling them what to do.

And besides being arrogant, telling people what to do is usually ineffective. Even if they comply, the change won't last unless it comes from within. It doesn't help to tell an addict that they should quit using, or an obese person that they should lose weight, or a guy who's being mean to his wife to be nice to her. I can offer help to people who really want to change, but they have to want the changes themselves.[80]

Except, every once in a while, someone like Edgar invites me to offer instructions, and I do, and it helps. Learning to not get carried away by my own theorizing has been an object lesson for me. Sometimes solutions are simple.

What happened to Edgar and Sharon? They—or I should say, couples like them in my actual practice—usually decided they were fine after another session or two. I don't argue with people's assessments of success for the same reasons that I don't (often) tell people what to do—it's not up to me to determine what people should want from therapy. I've also seen couples like Edgar and Sharon come back a few years later, but only rarely.

Wilma and George

Wilma and George (from Chapter 1) were no longer trying to be a couple when I met them; they were trying, ostensibly, to find ways to work together and co-parent more effectively. I've worked with many people in similar situations over the years, not always starting with the same level of animosity that Wilma and George showed toward each other (though it's not infrequent, either).

---

[80]How many therapists does it take to change a light bulb? Just one, but the light bulb has to really want to change.

In my experience, theirs is typically short-term work. The people involved usually don't want to do more than a session or two, and the work focuses narrowly on helping them to reduce their mutual reactivity so that they can cooperate. This is overwhelmingly about stability, and very little about intimacy.

I've seen some interesting exceptions, however. Occasionally I've worked with exes, sometimes together with their new partners, who have come to my office because they see the effects of their animosity on their children. They end up not only reducing their reactivity, but building cordial, and even warm, relationships. I don't know if that would have happened with a real Wilma and George, but it's helpful to know that it's possible.

Tara and Trey

We met Tara and Trey in Chapter 2, as an example of a couple that was having trouble maintaining stability in their relationship. They would argue, break up, get involved with others, get back together, rinse and repeat multiple times. Each of their childhoods shaped their tendency to panic when they sensed the other's disapproval, and their use of alcohol as their go-to method of self-soothing exacerbated that tendency.

As usual, the work with couples similar to Tara and Trey could go in various directions. Sometimes the partners each need to improve their emotional regulation skills before they can handle the anxiety of couples therapy—which is a fancy way of saying they freak out in sessions, or between sessions, too much to continue. If they discontinue therapy, I usually don't get to find out if they made it out of their breakup-makeup cycle.

But sometimes, at least one of the partners is able to get hold of themselves enough to escape the cycle. This often means that they address addiction issues, usually through individual therapy and/or a 12-step program. All it takes is for one of the partners to do this, and the relationship inevitably changes. Of course, this doesn't necessarily mean the relationship continues—often it means they break up. But if the relationship does continue—if it is no longer based on mutual reactivity—then it becomes possible to work on both stability and intimacy issues.

I've seen some couples who started out like Tara and Trey go on to not only escape the cycle, but build a strong relationship with each other. I've seen others who escape the cycle, break up with each other, and go on to develop strong relationships with other partners—which I discover because they might be back individually, or with their new partners, to work with me years later.

Doris and Ken

We also met Doris and Ken in Chapter 2. Their difficulty wasn't stability, but intimacy. They had been together for decades and had maintained a comfortable relationship, in part (it turned out) by avoiding issues that caused anxiety. What brought them to therapy was Ken's discovery of text messages between Doris and her old boyfriend. Both Doris and Ken recognized that the texts had crossed a line into the inappropriate, based on their understanding of fidelity. Ken felt Doris had cheated on him, and Doris didn't disagree with that characterization.

We followed Ken and Doris through several chapters because they were my example of a couple who manifested all three principles of the seven-word formula. They were kind, in the sense that they experienced a strong sense of kinship. That feeling was shaken by the crisis, but still strong nonetheless. They were able to tolerate the anxiety of the crisis without dissolving into panic. And they showed faith—which meant they each realized that what they were going through, painful though it may be, was meaningful. They were able to forgive themselves and each other, which is to say they got past the initial anger and recriminations to face their situation with courage and clarity.

Since Doris and Ken are essentially my poster couple for the seven words, I'd love to say that they (and real couples like them) inevitably went on to live happily ever after as a loving couple. That reflects a bias on my part, I realize, toward helping couples stay together—or more accurately, a bias against encouraging couples to split up, unless there are important reasons to do so. I've heard of many therapists (often from their clients) who do subtly or overtly encourage couples to split up, based on a view of therapy that privileges individual feelings over considerations of character, commitment, and moral judgment.[81] Of course, I recognize and honor each person's right to make their own decisions, and I know that the ability to break up is a crucial safety valve. But, as I described in Chapter 10 about marriage, I think being a couple is not just about the couple. Often, healing a couple is key to healing a family, a community, and a world.

So, as I noted above, I wish I could say that couples like Doris and Ken invariably heal and go on to enjoy years of satisfying marriage. But, of course, it's not always so. I've worked with many couples who do just that, but I've also worked with many who split up after an experience of infidelity, even if they've accomplished a lot of healing. Some cheated-on partners can forgive the offending partner, as Ken was able to do, but still find that their understanding of a monogamous relationship doesn't allow for staying together after a betrayal. They aren't angry with their partner anymore and might even have a compassionate understanding of why the cheating happened, but nevertheless decide to split up.

But whether they stay together or split up, couples like Doris and Ken report being better off as a result of the crisis. In that sense, they epitomize what the seven words are about.

Peter and Stella

Peter and Stella were introduced in Chapter 6 to illustrate the importance of getting to the right argument. They had been fighting about pretty much anything and everything, leading to a nasty set of exchanges that had them questioning if they could stay together.

In the course of our work, they realized that the fights had allowed them to avoid a scary possibility: that their respective visions of what they wanted for their lives might be fundamentally incompatible. When they were able to clarify that—to get to the right argument— they largely stopped squabbling and were able to regain some sense

---

[81]See, for example, Doherty (1997) for a discussion of this phenomenon.

of good will. That helped them to back away from desperation, but it didn't solve the problem. Whether they chose to stay together would depend on whether their differences, in the terms I used in Chapter 13, were deal-breakers or growing pains.

Variations on this theme are very common in my practice. I've seen it with long-married couples, as well as relatively new relationships. The fact that the situation often changes dramatically once a couple finds the right argument is a testimony to the power of intimate communication.

I've long since given up on predicting a couple's fate in terms of staying together or splitting up, but getting to the right argument is the way out of endless squabbling.[82] Whether Peter and Stella stayed together or not is uncertain, but they (and their many real counterparts) were better able to handle their situation once they stopped avoiding their scary dilemmas with pointless fighting.

John and Millie

We met John and Millie in Chapter 8, in our discussion of how faith helps a relationship. They were the contrast to Doris and Ken. As we noted above, Doris and Ken approached their very similar situation (the woman of the couple texting an old boyfriend inappropriately) with faith, accepting that the situation was meaningful, even though it was painful.

In contrast, John and Millie were determined to get back to how things were before, which meant that they couldn't see what Millie did as anything but a meaningless aberration. John's near-constant badgering of Millie was an attempt to somehow make it all go away. If only she could give just the right explanation, offer just the right reassurance, John would awaken from the nightmare. Of course, it never worked.

In some ways, John and Millie exemplify a process that nearly all couples dealing with infidelity seem to go through in the immediate aftermath of the discovery. John's actions correspond to

---

[82]I suppose that's a circular observation, since one indicator that a couple has found the right argument is that they stop squabbling.

the first four of Kübler-Ross's (1969) stages of grief: denial (refusing to believe it), anger (raging at Millie), bargaining ("just give me the right explanation and I'll stop hounding you"), and depression ("my life is ruined"). Presumably, Ken had similar reactions when he first found out about Doris's texting. But John and Millie hadn't yet made it to the fifth stage—acceptance—which, in terms of this book, is what faith is all about.

EPILOGUE

The Seven Words Revisited

As I mentioned in the Introduction, I first came up with my seven-word formula in response to a colleague, who asked me to summarize how I did couples therapy. What, in essence, do I tell people who come for therapy?

My first take on this question was five words: "Be kind and don't panic." When people panic, they often behave in ways that threaten their sense of kinship with each other. The central task of couples therapy, then, is to help people avoid panic, so they can regain and reinforce that sense of kinship for which they became a couple in the first place.

At first, the five-word formula seemed like a good summary of what couples therapy teaches people. The various therapeutic techniques I had learned were based on differing theoretical orientations, but they all seemed to be geared toward helping people avoid panic as they faced their problems.

But as I considered what actually seemed to help the couples I worked with, I realized that I needed to add two more words: "have faith." No matter what therapeutic techniques I used, the key to helping people not panic was to instill faith. The people who accepted reality as right, and therefore found meaning in their lives even as they struggled, were the people who healed. The couples that manifested faith were the couples who went on to have deep, satisfying relationships. Or, if they split up, they did so with mutual respect and compassion. The seven-word formula—"Be kind, don't panic, and have faith"—has guided my work ever since.

Throughout this book we've explored the three parts of the formula as they apply to couple relationships. We talked about kindness in the sense of kinship; we considered panic and how it affects a couple's ability to maintain that sense of kinship; and we discussed faith as the essential skill that lets people face their struggles without dissolving into panic. Along the way, we met some couples who exemplified those struggles.

Among the hundreds of actual couples I've worked with, I think most started out their therapy less like Doris and Ken, my poster couple for the power of faith, and more like John and Millie, who lost their sense of kinship in panic because they hadn't found their way to faith. Many of the couples I work with start out feeling desperately anxious. A couple in crisis isn't merely experiencing something painful; they're often sensing that their whole world is shaking, and they can't find stable ground. What they knew to be true no longer applies, especially regarding their sense of kinship with each other. It's no wonder that they often have a hard time accepting reality as right, pain and all.

If you're in that situation—or if you're a therapist helping couples in that situation—I hope this book has invited you to choose faith. When you can accept reality as right, and therefore meaningful, you can learn to calm your panic. And when you calm your panic, you can recover your sense of kinship, stop fighting, and work on healing.

Your Next Steps

What are your next steps? What work do you need to do now?

Perhaps you realize that you have unhealed trauma that is interfering with your ability to get hold of yourself, and you need to heal the trauma. Perhaps you want to graduate from plain old sex to good sex to sacred sex, so you need to expand your sexual repertoire and cultivate your sense of sacredness. Perhaps you want to propose marriage, or realize you don't want to, and you need to tell your partner how you feel. Perhaps you realize that you need to break up with your partner, or that you want to work on your problems together, and you need to make a decision.

Perhaps you recognize, for any of a host of reasons, that you could benefit from couples therapy, and you need to risk bringing it up with your partner. Or perhaps you just recognize the joys of stability and intimacy in your life, and you realize you're grateful.

Whatever work you need to do, I want to offer you a Jewish blessing: May you go *me-chayil el chayil*, from strength to strength.

Be kind, don't panic, and have faith. To be kind, you need to not panic, and to not panic, you need to have faith. That's what you need to know about relationships. Now get on with your work.

ACKNOWLEDGMENTS

I am grateful, first of all, to the many couples and individuals who have consulted me over the past three decades, from whom I have learned so much about the power of resilience, faith, and forgiveness. In addition to them, many colleagues, friends, and family members have helped shape the ideas in this book; in particular, I thank those who read and commented on various versions of the manuscript, including Judy Alexander, Eli Chalmer, Karen Chalmer, Seth Chalmer, Vicky Colvin, Christine DiBlasio, Lisa Harrington, Jennifer Levine, Bat Sheva Marcus, and Mark Pendergrast. Inclusion in that list doesn't mean agreement with everything I say.

Thanks also to Tom Corson-Knowles, Hannah Gordon, Kaelyn Barron, Sarah Dyck, and the production team at TCK Publishing for their skill, cordiality, and persistence in making this book happen, working to improve it, and teaching me how to let you know about it.

With all those people having looked over the book, any remaining errors couldn't possibly have been my fault, could they?

My wife, Judy Alexander, has taught me more than I would have thought possible about how deeply fulfilling a marriage can be. To her, my *y'did nefesh*, I dedicate this book.

ABOUT THE AUTHOR

Dr. Bruce Chalmer has been a psychologist working with couples for almost thirty years. Through his teaching, consulting, and videos about relationships, his ideas have helped thousands of couples and their therapists.

He has held leadership positions in some of Vermont's Jewish communities, and is also a musician and composer. He lives in South Burlington, Vermont, with his wife Judy Alexander. They have five adult children and four grandchildren.

CONNECT WITH

BRUCE

Sign up for Dr. Chalmer's blog at
www.askdrchalmer.brucechalmer.com

To find out more information visit his website:
www.brucechalmer.com

Facebook Pages:
www.facebook.com/drbrucechalmer
www.facebook.com/AskDrChalmer

BOOK DISCOUNTS
& SPECIAL DEALS

Sign up for free to get discounts and special deals
on our bestselling books at
www.TCKpublishing.com/bookdeals

REFERENCES

APA. (2019). Prolonged Exposure (PE). Retrieved from https://www.apa.org/ptsd-guideline/treatments/prolonged-exposure.aspx

Benedict, R. (1946). *The chrysanthemum and the sword: Patterns of Japanese culture.* New York, NY: Houghton Mifflin.

Brooks, D. (2015). *The road to character.* New York: Random House.

Buongiorno, J. & Notarius, C. (1992). *Wait time until professional treatment in marital therapy.* Unpublished master's thesis, Catholic University of America, Washington, DC.

Carroll, L. (1900). *Through the looking-glass and what Alice found there.* Chicago: W.B. Conkey Co.

Chalmer, B. (1986). *Understanding statistics.* New York: Marcel Dekker, Inc.

ChildTrends. (2018, September 24). *Births to unmarried women.* Retrieved from ChildTrends: https://www.childtrends.org/indicators/births-to-unmarried-women

De Waal, F. (2013, March). Has militant atheism become a religion? *Salon.* Retrieved from https://www.salon.com/2013/03/25/militant_atheism_has_become_a_religion/

Dickson, E. (2018, December 14). There's a stigma around lube. These brands want to change that. *Vox.* Retrieved from https://www.vox.com/the-goods/2018/12/14/18141193/lube-brands-stigma-personal-lubricant-ky-foria

Doherty, W. H. (1997). How therapists threaten marriages. *The Responsive Community*, 7, 31-42.

Domestic violence. (2002). *Encyclopedia of Crime and Justice.* Retrieved from https://www.encyclopedia.com/social-sciences-and-law/law/crime-and-law-enforcement/domestic-violence

Einstein, A. (1941). Science, philosophy and religion, a symposium . New York: Conference on Science, Philosophy and Religion in Their Relation to the Democratic Way of Life, Inc.

EMDR Institute, Inc. (2019). "What is EMDR". Retrieved from http://www.emdr.com/what-is-emdr/

Fetters, A. (2018, October 24). So is living together before marriage linked to divorce or what? *Atlantic*. Retrieved from https://www.theatlantic.com/family/archive/2018/10/premarital-cohabitation-divorce/573817/

Frost, R. (1920, December). Fire and Ice. *Harper's Magazine*, p. 67.

Goff, P. (2018, February 8). Is the universe a conscious mind? Retrieved from Aeon: https://aeon.co/essays/cosmopsychism-explains-why-the-universe-is-fine-tuned-for-life

Gottman, J. (2015). Principia amoris: The new science of love. New York: Routledge/Taylor & Francis Group.

Haidt, J. (2007). Moral psychology and the misunderstanding of religion. *Edge*. Retrieved from https://www.edge.org/conversation/jonathan_haidt-moral-psychology-and-the-misunderstanding-of-religion

Haidt, J. (2012). *The righteous mind*. New York, NY: Pantheon/Random House.

Hebb, D. (1949). *The organization of behavior: A neuropsychological theory*. New York, NY: Wiley & Sons.

Jarvis, D. (1958). *Folk medicine*. New York, NY: Holt.

Kelly, S. D. (2017, December 25). Waking up to the gift of "aliveness". *New York Times*. Retrieved from (https://www.nytimes.com/2017/12/25/opinion/aliveness-waking-up-holidays.html)

Kübler-Ross, E. (1969). *On death and dying*. London: Routledge.

Kuperberg, A. (2016, January 15). *Age at coresidence, premarital cohabitation, and marriage dissolution: 1985–2009*. Retrieved from NC Docks: http://libres.uncg.edu/ir/uncg/listing.aspx?styp=ti&id=17537

Kuusilehto, V. (2018). *"I'm very sorry to say that I've behaved badly":* *Image repair, public apologies and nonapologies during the Weinstein* *scandal.* University of Oulu. Retrieved from http://jultika.oulu.fi/ files/nbnfioulu-201805041585.pd

Lukianoff, G. and Haidt, J. (2018). *The coddling of the American mind.* New York: Penguin Press.

Mills, H., Reiss, N. & Dombeck, M. (2019). Stress inoculation therapy. *MentalHelp.net.* Retrieved from https://www.mentalhelp. net/articles/stress-inoculation-therapy/

National Center for Health Statistics. (2019). *Unmarried childbearing.* Retrieved from Centers for Disease Control and Prevention: https://www.cdc.gov/nchs/fastats/unmarried-childbearing.htm

National Center for PTSD. (2019). PTSD and substance abuse in veterans. Retrieved from https://www.ptsd.va.gov/understand/ related/substance_abuse_vet.asp

NORC. (2018). *GSS Data Explorer.* Retrieved from http:// gssdataexplorer.norc.org

Perel, E. (2006). *Mating in Captivity: Unlocking Erotic Intelligence.* New York: HarperCollins.

Perel, E. (2017). *The state of affairs: Rethinking infidelity.* New York, NY: Harper Collins.

Porges, S. (2009). The polyvagal theory: New insights into adaptive reactions of the autonomic nervous system. *Cleveland Clinic Journal of Medicine,* 76(Supplement 2), S86-S90.

Rao, S. (2018, January 11). He harassed her. She called him out. He broadcast his apology. She accepted. *Washington Post.* Retrieved from https://www.washingtonpost.com/news/ arts-and-entertainment/wp/2018/01/11/he-harassed-her-she- called-him-out-he-broadcast-his-apology-she-accepted/?utm_ term=.2ec9b4a47350

Sacks, J. (2011). *The great partnership: Science, religion, and the search for meaning.* New York: Schocken Books.

Sacks, J. (2012, October 10). *Bereishit (5773) - a living book*. Retrieved from Covenant and Conversation: http://rabbisacks. org/covenant-conversation-bereishit-the-living-book/

Sacks, J. (2016). The power of shame. Retrieved from http:// rabbisacks.org/the-power-of-shame-metsorah-5776/

SAMHSA - HRSA. (2019). *Trauma*. Retrieved from SAMHSA - HRSA Center for Integrated Health Studies: https://www. integration.samhsa.gov/clinical-practice/trauma

Schnarch, D. (2011). *Intimacy and desire: Awaken the passion in your relationship*. New York: Beaufort Books, Inc.

Schwartz, R. (1995). *Internal family systems therapy*. New York, NY: Guilford Press.

Smith, E. E. (2014, June 12). Masters of love. *Atlantic*. Retrieved from https://www.theatlantic.com/health/archive/2014/06/ happily-ever-after/372573/

Truth About Deception. (2019). *Facts and statistics about infidelity*. Retrieved from Truth About Deception: https://www. truthaboutdeception.com/cheating-and-infidelity/stats-about-infidelity.html

Washburn, A.N & Skitka, L.J. (2017). Science denial across the political divide: Liberals and conservatives are similarly motivated to deny attitude-inconsistent science. *Social Psychological and Personality Science*, 972-980.

White, M., & Epston, D. (1990). *Narrative means to therapeutic ends*. Adelaide, Australia: Dulwich Centre.

INDEX

Made in the USA
Middletown, DE
13 December 2022

18207082R00094